Bloom's

GUIDES

William Golding's
Lord of the Flies

CURRENTLY AVAILABLE

1984
All the Pretty Horses
Beloved
Brave New World
The Crucible
Cry, the Beloved Country
Death of a Salesman
Hamlet
The Handmaid's Tale
The House on Mango Street
I Know Why the Caged Bird Sings
Lord of the Flies
Macbeth
Maggie: A Girl of the Streets
Ragtime
The Scarlet Letter
Snow Falling on Cedars
To Kill a Mockingbird

Bloom's

GUIDES

William Golding's
Lord of the Flies

Edited & with an Introduction
by Harold Bloom

CHELSEA HOUSE
PUBLISHERS

A Haights Cross Communications Company

Philadelphia

First Printing
1 3 5 7 9 8 6 4 2

Library of Congress Cataloging-in-Publication Data
Applied for.
ISBN 0-7910-7878-7

Chelsea House Publishers
1974 Sproul Road, Suite 400
Broomall, PA 19008-0914

www.chelseahouse.com

Contributing editor: Pamela Loos
Cover design by Takeshi Takahashi
Layout by EJB Publishing Services

Contents

39755

Introduction

HAROLD BLOOM

The survival of *Lord of the Flies* (1954) half a century after its initial publication, is not in itself a testimony to the book's permanence, even as a popular fiction of the boy's adventure story genre. Golding, a schoolmaster for many years, clearly knew a good deal about the psychology of young boys, particularly in regard to group dynamics. Whether the psychological representations of *Lord of the Flies* remain altogether convincing seems to me rather questionable; the saintly Simon strains credibility as a naturalistic portrait. In many ways the book is remarkably tendentious, and too clearly has a program to urge upon us. Overt moral allegory, even in a lively adventure story, may arouse our resentments, and I find it difficult to reread *Lord of the Flies* without a certain skepticism towards Golding's designs upon his reader. In some sense, the book is Mark Twain turned upside down, and I mean the Mark Twain of *Roughing It* rather than of *Adventures of Huckleberry Finn*. Sometimes I like to try the critical experiment of pretending to be Mark Twain as I read *Lord of the Flies*. How *would* Huck Finn have reacted to the regressive saga of the English school-boys of *Lord of the Flies*? We cannot find any trace of Huck in Ralph or in Jack, in Simon or in Piggy or in Roger. Golding, I think, would have been furious at my suggestion that this has something to do with Huck's being American, and Golding's boys being British. Original Sin is not a very American idea, and the wonderful skepticism of Huck, at any age, would have preserved him from being either an implausible saint or a bestial hunter. This is hardly to suggest that we are less savage or violence-prone than the British; Huck knows better, and we know better. But it may indicate some of the limitations of *Lord of the Flies*; as a grim fable, unrelieved in its rigor, it lacks all humor, and is an involuntary parody of Twain's *Roughing It* or his *Innocents Abroad*.

Golding once said that the dead parachutist in *Lord of the Flies* was meant to represent "History," in the adult sense. The moral implication that Golding intended doubtless was that the group reversion to organized savagery in his book was no different from adult reversion, at any time. Whether a reader finds this convincing seems to me quite disputable: an American might want to reply, with Ralph Waldo Emerson, that there is no history, only biography. Golding's fable is vivid and is narrated with great skill, but is it a fable of universal relevance? At the end, Golding tells us that "Ralph wept for the end of innocence, the darkness of man's heart." Are we moved by Ralph's weeping, or do we flinch at it because of Golding's inverted sentimentalism? Emotion in excess of the object that provokes it tends to be a pragmatic definition of sentimentality. I suspect that it comes down to the issue of universalism: do the boys of *Lord of the Flies* represent the human condition, or do they reflect the traditions of British schools with their restrictive structures, sometimes brutal discipline, and not always benign visions of human nature? Golding himself said that society, whether in life or in *Lord of the Flies*, plays only a minor role in bringing about human violence and depravity. But what about the one society his boys truly have known, the society of their schools? One can admire *Lord of the Flies* as a tale of adventure, while wondering whether its moral fable was not far more insular than Golding seems to have realized.

Biographical Sketch

William Gerald Golding was born on September 19, 1911 to Mildred Golding, an activist for women's suffrage, and Alec Golding, a mathematics teacher and eventual senior master at Marlborough Grammar School. Golding led a somewhat isolated childhood, spent largely in the company of his nurse Lily. He attended Marlborough Grammar School and in 1930 he entered Brasenose College, Oxford to study science but soon switched to English literature. While at college, a friend sent twenty-nine of Golding's poems to Macmillan; his *Poems* was published in the Contemporary Poets series. In 1935 he received a BA in English and diploma in education from Oxford, and then became a social worker at a London settlement house. Golding wrote, acted, and produced for a small, noncommercial theater in London in his spare time. In 1939 he married Ann Brookfield, an analytical chemist; they had a son and a daughter. The same year he was married Golding began teaching English, Greek literature in translation, and philosophy at Bishop Wordsworth's School in Salisbury. He was involved in adult education, teaching in army camps and Maidstone Gaol.

Golding enlisted in the Royal Navy at the start of World War II. He achieved the rank of lieutenant and was given command of a small rocket-launching craft in which he was involved in the chase and sinking of the *Bismarck*; he also participated in the D-Day assault in 1944. After the war, Golding returned to Bishop Wordsworth's school where he would teach for the next 16 years. In 1954, *Lord of the Flies* was published by Faber and Faber after being rejected by twenty-one other publishers. Because the book was an immediate success in England and an eventual best-seller in the United States, Golding was able to retire from teaching in order to pursue his writing career full time. *The Inheritors*, a tale of savagery about the extermination of the Neanderthals by the Homo Sapiens in pre-historic times, was published in 1955. Many critics deemed this novel superior to *Lord of the Flies*.

Shortly after its publication Golding became a fellow of the Royal Society of Literature. In 1956, *Pincher Martin* was published, and subsequently republished in the United States as *The Two Lives of Christopher Martin*. His play, *The Brass Butterfly*, was performed at Oxford and in London in 1958, and *Free Fall* was published in 1959. Golding's novels of the 1950s established him as one of the leading voices in British fiction.

Between 1960-62 Golding becomes a frequent contributor of essays and book reviews to the *Spectator*. In 1960 he completed his Master of Arts degree at Brasenose College, and the year after Golding spent as writer in residence at Hollins College, Virginia, and toured as a lecturer at other American Colleges. In 1963 *Lord of the Flies* was produced for film, and *The Spire* was published in 1964. A collection of essays, *The Hot Gates* was published in 1965, and Golding was made a Commander of the British Empire (CBE). In 1966 he became an honorary fellow of Brasenose College, Oxford and the following year *The Pyramid*, a collection of novellas, was published. Golding was awarded an honorary doctor of letters by Sussex University in 1970 and *The Scorpion God: Three Short Novels* was published the year after.

After a period of eight years in which no new work would be published by Golding, he experienced a critical resurgence with the publication of *Darkness Visible* in 1979, *Rites of Passage* in 1980, which won the Booker Prize for fiction, and a second collection of essays, *A Moving Target* in 1982. In 1983 Golding reached the pinnacle of his career, receiving the Nobel Prize for Literature.

Golding continued to produce new works throughout the 1980s, publishing *The Paper Men* (1984), *An Egyptian Journal* (1985), *Close Quarters* (1987), the second volume of the sea trilogy begun with *Rites of Passage*, and *Fire Down Below* (1989), the conclusion of the trilogy. In 1990 a new film version of *Lord of the Flies* was produced. William Golding died on June 19, 1993 at Perranarworthal. A draft of his novel *The Double Tongue*, left at the time of his death, was published posthumously in 1995.

The Story Behind the Story

Although William Golding initially planned to become a poet, that goal changed after the publication in 1954 of his first novel, *Lord of the Flies*. Considered by some to be his greatest work, it unquestionably is the novel that brought him the most attention. Read in many classrooms, the novel also has been made into a movie, and Golding received many letters about his book—from teachers, students, parents, psychiatrists, psychologists, and clergy, for example. Its accessibility and disturbing but vital message attracted readers in the aftermath of World War II and has continued to do so for decades later, when to many the world still appears a place of brutality and instability. The response to the work inspired Golding to give up poetry and stay with novel writing; while his first published book had been a collection of poems, he later said he didn't even own a copy of it.

Golding fought in World War II, and when the war was finally over, he saw that people were still shocked about how Hitler and his regime inflicted such large-scale inhumane horrors on the Jews and others. Golding felt compelled to write about man's evil. But beyond this, he wanted to make it clear in his book that such behavior could occur anywhere, even in a seemingly advanced nation such as England. "The overall picture," Golding wrote about *Lord of the Flies*, "was to be the tragic lesson that the English have had to learn over a period of one hundred years; that one lot of people is inherently like any other lot of people; and that the only enemy of man is inside him." Golding wrote that the concept was really not new but people desperately needed to be reminded of it.

Golding also wrote about another concept he included in *Lord of the Flies*, what he called "off-campus history." Off-campus history, he explained, is different from academic history, which is taught in schools. It is a deep resentment handed down from generation to generation about a certain group or groups of people. He provided the example of a

11

French woman who saw her country conquered in 1870, 1914, and 1940, and as a result had developed such an intense hatred for Germans that she shook whenever she thought of them. In Golding's novel, the parachutist, which some readers saw as a symbol that God is dead, was meant to stand for off-campus history, "the thing which threatens every child everywhere, the history of blood and intolerance, of ignorance and prejudice, the thing which is dead but won't lie down."

Due to the popularity of *Lord of the Flies*, Golding also described his other motivations behind writing it and decisions he made about the content and story. For example, having been one of a mass of English schoolboys who read Robert Ballantyne's idealized island adventure book *Coral Island*, Golding explained that he wanted to write a realistic alternative to it. In the Ballantyne book, as the critic James Baker has written, "everything comes off in exemplary style." The boys master their island environment, they use "sheer moral force" to easily defeat pirates, and use Christianity to readily convert and reform the cannibal inhabitants. Published in 1858, *Coral Island* maintained great popularity, and Golding incorporated a number of its characteristics in his novel so as to satirize it and other books like it. Golding even had characters in *Lord of the Flies* specifically mention *Coral Island*. Early in Golding's book, when the characters are still excited about being on the beautiful island, they mention *Coral Island*, hopeful that they can mimic its atmosphere. Also, at the very end of *Lord of the Flies*, the officer who rescues the boys is shocked that English boys could behave so poorly. When Ralph tries to explain that in the beginning things were running smoothly, the officer helps him out by saying it was like the Coral Island. The contrast between what happened on Coral Island and what happens in *Lord of the Flies* is severe. And while the contrast between how life is at the beginning of *Lord of the Flies* and how it is at the end is also severe, it is even more disturbing, since the very same boys act so very differently in a relatively short period of time. Not only do they kill other boys, but their desire to kill leads them to set such a destructive fire on the island that they are destroying even their own source of protection and food; destruction seems to know no limits.

Regarding the ending of *Lord of the Flies*, Golding has explained that at the time he wrote the novel he believed that saving the character of Ralph was the only way to provide the opportunity for him to become self-aware (although his awareness provokes despair). This mix of hope and despair seems fitting for Golding, who in a 1964 interview observed, "I think that democratic attitude of voluntary curbs put on one's own nature is the only possible way for humanity, but I wouldn't like to say that it's going to work out, or survive."

List of Characters

Ralph is twelve years old, fair-haired, and attractive. Although he is readily elected chief, he still needs the help of Piggy's intelligence. His differentness provokes the boys to elect him, and his actions in the position are what prompt the reader to believe there is hope that practicality and civility can exist, even among youngsters left to care for themselves in the wild. His mistreatment of Piggy and his joining in the violence against Simon show how easily it is for even the good to succumb to evil.

Piggy is intelligent and sensitive, yet because of other, mostly physical characteristics, he is ultimately overpowered. He was raised by his aunt, is overweight, has asthma, cannot swim, and is the only boy who wears glasses. As intelligent as he is, he misjudges the evil of the others, believing they can be spoken with rationally and never realizes the seriousness of the situation and the potential for a deathly response. He stands as the example of the power of intelligence, strong enough to overcome many flaws but not strong enough to overcome a blind spot about understanding human nature.

Jack Merridew is the only boy who, early in the book, says he wants to be called by his last name. (In fact, only his and one other boy's last names are given.) He has red hair, an unpleasant face, and demands control over the choir boys he is placed in charge of in school. He is quick to show that he carries a large knife, almost never backs down from confrontation, and is excited about having an "army" of hunters, and about having rules because he anticipates the pleasure of punishing those who will break them. Ironically, he is the rule breaker who splits from the group, forces others to join him, and becomes more and more evil. He shows how easily evil gains power.

Simon, a member of the choir, is sensitive, quiet, and prone to fainting. He wishes he could speak publicly to the boys and be accepted by Ralph and his group, who for the most part think him "batty." He needs time to be alone, is quite brave and giving, and understands humanity. Golding has called him the Christ figure of the book, since he has a rather mystical communication with evil, a message for the boys, and becomes a martyr, although some critics have taken issue with this.

Sam and Eric are twins who function as if they are indistinguishable from each other. As a result, often they are referred to as "Samneric." They know each other's thoughts, complete each other's sentences, and are always together. Early on they appear somewhat irresponsible when they abandon their key post at the fire and childish when they make fun of Ralph to each other. Yet later in the book they are quite loyal to Ralph and want to do what is right.

Roger is another choir member who is brave enough to climb the mountain with Jack and Ralph to search for the beast. His mischief against younger boys in the book's beginning is just a precursor to the danger he inflicts by throwing stones and then launching the largest rock of all as a weapon. Unlike many of the others, he doesn't need Jack to provoke his evil side.

Maurice, Bill, and **Robert,** are the other older boys from the choir who join Jack's group. Initially, like the other choir members, they are imposing for the black robes they wear as well as their black caps. Ironically, the choir members are the only ones described as wearing crosses and yet are the first to join Jack's evil "tribe" (except for Simon). Later they don the "savage" war paint, hunt, and follow Jack's orders. They are mentioned by name only a few times, and are not given distinct personalities, except perhaps for Maurice, who a few times shows he understands how to defuse a tense situation but also seemingly foolishly increases the fear in the little ones because of his comments at a meeting. These boys are an example of the danger of followers.

The **"littluns"** (short for "little ones") are the youngest of the boys, each being roughly six years old, and are usually not differentiated as individuals. They can be playful but are plagued with fearful fantasies and nightmares. Since they are so young, they can contribute little and to some degree must be taken care of.

Percival Wemys Madison is a littlun who is prone to crying and who prompts other small ones to do so as well. When asked for his name, he gives his full name and address, but only part of his phone number. Apparently he had been quite practiced in reciting this before arriving on the island. Now unable to remember what his parents must have carefully trained him in and emphasized as important, he is another symbol of the breakdown of civilization on the island. When he says the beast comes from the sea, he inspires chaos at a meeting, indicating the ease with which fear overtakes most of the group.

The **boy with the wine-colored scar** is a littlun who first makes public his own and the other young ones' fears of a beast. He becomes a symbol of what happens when accountability is not taken by those who should be responsible.

Summary and Analysis

At the beginning of *Lord of the Flies*, we read of a fair-haired boy, who is dragging his school sweater and sweating as he attempts to make his way over rocks and through a rough hot jungle toward a lagoon. A voice calls to this boy to wait, which he does as he pulls up his "stockings with an automatic gesture that made the jungle seem for a moment like the Home Counties," the group of counties nearest London. Out of the undergrowth appears another boy, who's shorter than the first, very fat, and wearing thick eyeglasses and a "greasy wind-breaker," despite the heat.

The squat boy asks for the man with the megaphone but he is told that there is no such man, and that they are on an island; it seems that there may be no grownups on the island at all. The possibility that there are no grownups is disturbing to the younger boy, but the older one finds it so delightful that he stands on his head, grinning for a moment. The younger boy is rather unfazed by the other and continues to ponder the situation. The reader, like these boys, must piece together what has happened. Through the boys' dialogue, alternately overly optimistic and realistic, we learn that these boys and others were in a plane crash. The nose of the plane went down in flames, but the cabin landed in a seeming sweep through the jungle trees and then near enough to the water to be pulled out to sea, perhaps with some boys still aboard.

The smaller boy asks the other what his name is, and the taller boy says his name is Ralph, but doesn't ask the smaller boy for his name in return. Ralph starts again toward the lagoon, now going faster, slowing only because he trips. The smaller boy's breathing is more strained from trying to keep up, and he tells Ralph that his auntie has told him not to run since he has asthma. Ralph makes fun of the boy's improper pronunciation, but we realize he speaks grammatically incorrect as well.

While Ralph is described as standing among "skull-like coconuts," he remains enthralled with the freedom of the island, removes all of his clothes in glee, and is nearly entranced by the beach and water that they have reached. The author now tells us that Ralph is twelve, and while he has the physique of a boxer he hasn't the "devil" in him. Again he stands on his head in delight as the other young boy ponders their situation; the younger one says that they will have to learn all the others' names (another hint to Ralph that he still doesn't know this boy's name) and that they should have a meeting. Finally he tells Ralph that he just doesn't want anyone to call him the name they called him at school, which, he whispers, was "Piggy." At this, Ralph laughs wildly, dances, and pretends he is a fighter-plane attacking Piggy. Piggy actually takes some pleasure in the attention but repeats that Ralph can't tell the others.

The two boys explore a little further and find a raised jetty, with shade and an enchanting beach pool with warm water, glittering fish, and coral. Ralph plunges in with delight, and Piggy sticks one toe in tentatively. Ralph continues to stand out as the more fortunate boy. He learned to swim, whereas Piggy couldn't because of his asthma; Ralph's dad is a commander in the Navy, whereas Piggy's dad is dead and his mother was not around to raise him.

While Piggy's weaknesses seem almost in excess, he is quite intelligent and practical. When Ralph boyishly boasts that his father will come and rescue them, Piggy asks how he will find them, and Ralph scavenges for an answer that Piggy reminds him is impossible. Ralph's dad wouldn't be told by the people at the airport where the boys are, Piggy says. He questions Ralph: "Didn't you hear what the pilot said? About the atom bomb? They're all dead." This finally is enough to bring Ralph out of his idyllic daydreaming, and he literally pulls himself out of the delightful water and ponders the situation. Piggy persists in making it clear that no one knows where the boys are, meaning they may stay there until they die. The heat seems to greatly intensify, and Ralph again shows his return to reality by getting dressed.

Piggy insists that they find the others and "do something," but Ralph has already returned to his dreaming. He spies a conch shell in the water, and as Piggy expounds on its value, Ralph manuevers to get it. When Piggy warns him to be careful, Ralph "absently" tells him to "shut up," pointing to the contrast between each boy's level of concern for the other. Curiously, though, as much as Ralph feels that Piggy is interrupting his bliss, Piggy's intentness on sticking by Ralph's side makes sense. One way this is proven is by the fact that although Ralph is the one that sees the shell and determines a way to reach it, he still needs Piggy's help.

Piggy realizes that by blowing into the shell they can alert the others, indicating the significance of the chapter's title, "The Sound of the Shell." Piggy knows the technique for getting the shell to sound, but Ralph blows into it since Piggy has asthma. It takes a few tries on Ralph's part, but then the shell's "deep, harsh note boomed" and grew into "a strident blare," scattering birds and other wild animals and achieving the goal of alerting the others. A boy of about six is the first to appear; Piggy helps him to the platform and asks him his name, as Ralph continues sounding the shell. While the shell so far, even in its white appearance, has seemed only a positive image, Ralph's "face was dark with the violent pleasure" of making it bellow, indicating not necessarily that the shell itself is evil but that Ralph has a dark side, perhaps.

Piggy greets each child that appears and tries to memorize each one's name. They sit on the fallen tree trunks expectantly and are described as giving Piggy "the same simple obedience that they had given to the men with megaphones." This is the second vague reference to the power of the men with megaphones, but now that we know there has been an atomic blast we theorize that the men may have been responsible for evacuating the children before the attacks began. Aside from the first boy's name, Johnny, the only other names mentioned are those of the twins who appear, Sam and Eric, who also have light hair like Ralph. They are energetic, grinning, and nearly identical, and when Piggy tries to get their names straight but makes a mistake, the whole group laughs.

Yet there is an unusual black "creature" also approaching the platform, which Ralph is the first to spot. As it gets closer, the boys see that it is actually a group of boys dressed in eccentric black cloaks and caps, each cap having a silver badge. They are marching in twos behind "[t]he boy who controlled them," who also is dressed in this odd way but has a golden badge on his cap. He is tall and thin, yet has red hair and a "crumpled" face that is "ugly without silliness." His eyes are described as "turning, or ready to turn, to anger," and he is the first of his group to approach the gathered boys, making his cloaked boys, who we find out are choir members, wait several yards back. One boy faints, we assume from the heat, but then are told that this is commonplace for him.

Piggy is intimidated and moves to Ralph's side furthest away from this group and nervously wipes his glasses. The choir boys refer to their leader as Merridew, and he asks those gathered whether there are grown-ups on the island. They explain that there aren't and that they've called a meeting to get everyone's name and decide what to do next. Merridew scoffs at the collecting of first names, calling it childish and insisting he be called by his last name; throughout the rest of the book, though, he's called Jack. He tells Piggy he's talking too much, adding, "Shut up, Fatty," and provoking laughter from the others. Unfortunately the laughter only increases when Ralph tells the group Piggy's real name.

The decision is made to appoint Ralph chief, since he is tall, attractive, and has possession of the delicate yet powerful conch shell; he is described as having "a stillness" about him. To be fair, Ralph asks for those who would rather have Jack as chief to raise their hands; only the choir does, with "dreary obedience." Curiously, Piggy shows the same lack of enthusiasm when he and all the others raise their hands for Ralph. We find out a little later that he is crushed by Ralph having asked the others to call him "Piggy" when he had specifically asked Ralph not to.

The new chief decides that the first order of business is to determine if, in fact, they are on an island. Ralph says that he, Jack, and Simon, the boy who fainted, will explore, while everyone else stays there together. Jack draws some attention when he shows his large sheath-knife. Piggy wants to go but is turned away.

The three boys set off, happy and laughing excitedly, and Ralph again joyfully stands on his head. After walking to the end of the island, Ralph decides it's best to climb the mountain. The boys notice tracks, and Jack says they are from animals. Ralph, curious about them, "peered into the darkness under the trees. The forest minutely vibrated." It is an ominous description, yet the author tells us just this and nothing of the boys' reactions. As they get to the toughest part of their climb, they are awed, to be exploring where perhaps no one else has ever been. Since in this terrain Ralph cannot stand on his head, his usual exuberant action, he instead starts a fun scuffle with the others. The action seems innocuous enough, and certainly boyish, yet it also is an indication of trouble to come.

As the three near the top of the rocky incline, Jack notices a huge, loose rock. He calls for the others to help him push, and the rock finally moves through the air and then smashes into the forest below that shakes "as with the passage of an enraged monster." It is a destructive move, but the boys think it great fun and revel in their triumph.

Finally at the top, they see many butterflies and a lavish hanging blue flower that spreads down into the forest canopy. The boys find that they were indeed right in their assumption that they are on an island, and Ralph announces that it all belongs to them. They observe the island's rough boat-like shape, its coral reef, the gash where their plane has landed, and the platform where they have left the other boys, who now appear as mere insects.

Again they feel like triumphant friends. They see no signs of other humans, and Jack is excited about finding food, and hunting and catching "things" until they are rescued. Hearing this, the boys realize they are hungry, begin scrambling down the rocks, and then stop near the beginning of the forest when they come across a piglet trapped in the tangled growth. Jack had just moments before daringly slashed his knife into a beautiful flower, and now raises it again against this small struggling creature. When he hesitates, however, they realize the "enormity" of killing, and the animal gets away. Jack is white and provides excuses for why he didn't stab the pig. He promises that next time will be different and slams his knife into a tree trunk.

The three boys return to the others in **chapter 2**. It is now afternoon, and they reassemble when they hear Ralph blow the conch. Golding's interplay of light and dark is evident here as the older boys, who were not part of the choir, stand to the right of Ralph illuminated by the sun. The former choirboys, who have discarded their robes, stand to the left of Ralph in the dark. Ralph is somewhat uncomfortable in his chief role and gets no help from Piggy now, but when he starts to speak he immediately realizes the words flow freely and clearly.

Ralph reveals their discoveries: that they are on an island that appears to be uninhabited. With this, Jack interrupts to say an "army" is needed for hunting. Then all three boys speak of the trapped pig they saw and Jack again slams his knife into a tree, vowing to kill the next one they see.

Ralph announces also that, as in school, if someone wants to speak he must raise his hand. He will then give the boy the conch shell and he alone will speak without interruption from anyone but Ralph. At the very moment that he is explaining how they will avoid interruptions, Jack interrupts, jubilant, with thoughts of punishing those who break the new rules.

Piggy takes the shell and says Ralph has more to say, something that is most important. Like an expert orator, he pauses to increase their interest and tells them that no one knows where they are, since they never arrived at their final destination. Their plane was shot down in flames before they made it, and they may not be rescued for a long time. The group is silent, and then Ralph grins and explains the great positives about their situation; it's like being in a book, he says, and they all become excited.

A very small boy about six years old is pushed out from the group sitting in front of Ralph so that he can speak. Only after much prodding does he come forward, but Piggy must lean over and listen to him and then do the talking for him. The boy wants to know what they plan to do about the very large "snake-thing" that he saw in the woods, what he calls a "beastie." With this, the platform becomes cooler, either from the setting sun or from the varied breezes. The boys are disturbed.

Ralph explains that there is no such thing, but the little boy persists in his story and the others are grave, calmed only when Jack says that if there is such a thing they will hunt it down and kill it. Ralph is annoyed and frustrated and yells that this creature is an impossibility, and all are grimly silent. He shifts to speaking about the positive—they will be saved, since the queen has a map of every island in the world. All are relieved and applaud loudly, with Ralph feeling triumphant.

He tells them that to be saved they must make a fire on the top of the mountain, and at once they get up, with Jack joining in and calling for them to follow him. (The chapter's name is "Fire on the Mountain.") Ralph and Piggy are left, with Piggy perturbed by the others acting "like a crowd of kids!" This is one of the earliest indications that he does not understand human nature. He is surprised when Ralph rushes off after the boys as well, but then he too follows with the conch.

All but Piggy scavenge for materials to fuel the fire, only to realize that they don't know how to start a fire without matches. Jack says they can use Piggy's glasses and snatches them. The fire roars quickly, and the boys race for more wood, but it seems impossible to keep up, and the fire dies. Ralph says that the fire was no good anyway, since it was all flame and no smoke, which is what will get the attention of a passing ship. Piggy, still with the conch, chimes in, but Jack cuts him off. Piggy keeps trying to speak, but then Ralph takes the shell and says they must appoint groups to look after the fire. He says, too, that wherever the conch is there is a meeting.

Jack takes the shell and gives his hearty endorsement, again advocating rules: "After all, we're not savages. We're English, and the English are best at everything. So we've got to do the right things." He says that the choir, his hunters, will take responsibility for the fire and keep a lookout.

Piggy takes the shell, still trying to be heard, but then stops when he looks "down the unfriendly side of the mountain," since the fire is spreading there rapidly. The boys cheer as they watch it take over, and Ralph recognizes that they are becoming silent out of awe at the power they've unleashed. "The knowledge and the awe," Golding writes, "made him [Ralph] savage." Ralph yells for Piggy to shut up. Piggy is hurt but stands up for his right to speak since he has the conch. All are still intent on the fire as Piggy tries to get their attention then calls to Ralph, himself entranced by "the splendid, awful sight." Piggy chastises them for not acting properly, warning that this will keep them from being rescued. He also says the little kids were never all counted, since they had run amok when Ralph, Jack, and Simon had left and Piggy was supposed to have taken their names.

Ralph is angry, but the situation becomes even worse when Piggy says that some of the "littluns" are in the area where the fire has now spread to. He gasps for breath as he says that he doesn't see the little boy who had been so worried about the snakes. He is interrupted yet again, this time by a tree exploding in flames, provoking the little boys to scream as they see the creepers move into view. Piggy falls, gasping, asking again where this little boy is; the group is incredulous, and the fire continues.

Chapter 3 takes place some time later, since we're told that Jack's hair is now noticeably longer and that some meetings have taken place. The chapter opens with Jack hunting by himself, bent down, "dog-like," now with a long spear and wearing only tattered shorts. Compelled to kill, Jack seems a practiced hunter yet he is very frustrated with his lack of success; his eyes "seem bolting and nearly mad." He throws his spear yet misses a pig, and after a day of hunting, now full of sweat from the oppressive heat, he goes back to the rest of the boys for a break.

At this point, frustration is consuming Ralph as well. Jack sees him attempting to create shelters with Simon. Two shaky ones are up, but a third has just fallen. Ralph, like Jack, has to stop his task, and when he sees Jack he complains that the twice-a-day meetings don't seem to be working, that rather than helping with the shelters the boys only work for five minutes and go off to play, swim, eat, or go hunting. Jack is quick to remind him that they want meat, but Ralph says they need shelters, that the hunters left Jack hours ago and that they haven't caught anything yet anyway. There is madness in Jack's eyes as he tries to explain his compulsion to kill, but Ralph is insistent about the shelters, and both boys become quite angry.

Ralph turns away and changes the subject, explaining that there is another reason that the shelters are important. He looks into Jack's "fierce, dirty face" and tells him that the youngest boys (who they now regularly call the "littluns") as well as some of the older boys are thoroughly frightened and talk and scream as they dream during the night. Simon breaks in and says it appears the boys no longer realize that this is a "good island," as if they truly believe in the "beastie," which no one has mentioned since the first little boy did (who we assume was killed in the fire). Ralph echoes Simon's words about the island being a good one, but Jack, the one intent on killing and less aware of the others' needs, doesn't. He says the frightened boys are "batty," and Ralph agrees for the moment. The two boys grin as they recall the "glamour" of their first day exploring on the island.

Even so, Ralph says they need the shelters, and Jack shows he understands by finishing Ralph's sentence: they need the shelters as a kind of home. Indeed, the shelters are important to Golding as well, since the chapter is entitled, "Huts on the Beach."

Curiously, though, Jack is not as fearless as he appears. He explains that when he's hunting by himself "you can feel as if you're not hunting, but—being hunted, as if something's behind you all the time in the jungle.... That's how you can feel in the forest. Of course there's nothing in it. Only—only—." Ralph is incredulous but controls his reaction.

Meanwhile, Simon, whom Ralph has just described as odd to Jack, has gone off by himself. He is amid the acres of fruit trees, plentiful with fruit, flowers, and bees. He helps the littluns who follow him get the best fruit they cannot reach and continues to do so until all are satisfied. Again he goes off by himself to a small hidden spot in the jungle and stays there as evening approaches. The white flowers he had been intrigued by and described as candle-like on their first day on the island, while the others had seen no use for them, open in the starlight, with their aroma encompassing the entire island.

Chapter 4 continues with a description of nature. The morning is good on the island, but, we are told, "Strange things happened at midday." For example, mirages appear on the horizon as if a bump of land. They disappear at the end of the afternoon, which also brings coolness but starts the menacing journey toward darkness, which we already know causes fear in many of the boys.

We are told that the "littluns," each roughly six years old, live rather separately from the older boys. They have decorated sandcastles along the little river, and one day three are playing and interrupted by two of the bigger boys, Roger and Maurice, who destroy the castles on the way to the beach. Even though no adults are anywhere nearby, Maurice feels some twinge of guilt for causing the destruction, whereas Roger seems not to and is described as someone who initially seemed unsociable but now appears "forbidding."

Roger is not content with the small interference he caused. Rather than jumping into the water for his swim, he follows the biggest of the three boys, Henry, that had been playing and proceeds to tease him. Henry has now moved away from the other two young boys, fascinated by the miniscule scavengers that come in with the waves. Yet even this is a disturbing pastime, for Henry is making small ruts and paths in the sand and is thrilled to be controlling the creatures' movements by doing so, excited by the "illusion of mastery."

Roger throws stones at the involved Henry, but aims to miss, still abiding by the rules of his old life, even though, Golding writes, it is "a civilization that knew nothing of him and was in ruins." These passages produce strong forebodings. While there is some hope that civility is still possible, since even the most forbidding of the boys is not willing to cause too much harm, the question arises as to whether such a boy will still react the same way when he finds out that most of the outside world is ruined, or whether he will react the same way after being stuck on the island for a longer time.

Roger is called away by Jack, who has a new innovation that should help in their hunting. With Jack are three other older boys, the twins Sam and Eric, and Bill. Jack takes colored clay that he's found and paints his face, explaining that this will make it harder for the pigs to discern him in the brush. Jack is thrilled with his face-painting, and as he dances his laughter transforms into "bloodthirsty snarling." The face almost takes on its own life, and at the same time it hides the true Jack, now "liberated from shame and self-consciousness." The face repulses Bill to the point where he laughs, grows quiet and then leaves, but the face compels the twins, after some protest, to follow Jack to meet with the others preparing to surround a pig. It is unclear whether Roger goes with them.

The chapter is called "Painted Faces and Long Hair"; while only one boy has painted his face with the stark colors so far, almost all of the other boys are rather frequently described as pushing their long hair back from their foreheads. The unkempt hair makes them appear less civilized, but beyond this its growth is something out of their control, leading one to the idea that becoming less civilized is out of their control as well. Additionally, it hangs in their eyes, presumably making them increasingly blind. It is something that afflicts all of them except Piggy, whose hair remains wispy and never seems to grow.

We return to Ralph, who is unaware of what's going on with the older boys; he is just out of the bathing pool and followed by Piggy. To Ralph, Piggy is boring and fat, but there is pleasure to be derived from teasing him. When Piggy sees Ralph smile at this thought he's happy for what he believes is a sign of friendliness, especially since he's usually seen as an outsider because of his weight, eyeglasses, asthma, lack of assisting with manual labor, and accent, the last of which "did not matter," Golding tells us. The reader has already witnessed various treatments of Piggy, yet never have we had the commentary from Golding that Piggy's accent, specifically, did not matter. At least one critic disagrees with Golding and has commented that the accent, in fact, is chiefly what effects Piggy's treatment, for it is a trait that society frequently sees as a factor when differentiating classes, whereas Piggy's other faults could more easily affect people in any class.

What seems an average moment on the beach turns serious when Ralph jumps up and hollers that he sees smoke far out at sea. All the other boys clamour to the sand to look, while Piggy looks at the top of the mountain and asks if they, in fact, are producing any smoke signal. Ralph again is shown as the one who has to do the work; not only has he spotted the ship at sea but when the others are doubtful about the status of their own smoke, he is the first to start madly scrambling up the mountain. When he is partially up the side, cursing, Ralph realizes they will need Piggy's glasses if the fire is out, but Piggy is far behind. Ralph presses onward despite this, and upon reaching the top finds that the fire is out and those responsible for it are gone. He screams insanely and repeatedly for the ship to come back.

Bitterly angry, Ralph spots Jack and some of the others approaching them, including the twins, who, we learn, were supposed to have been on duty for the fire but are now carrying the carcass of a pig on a stake. The scantily dressed boys, some in black caps, are chanting, and only as they get closer can Ralph and the others make it out: "Kill the pig. Cut her throat. Spill her blood."

Jack reaches the mountaintop first. He and all the others are excited to tell how they cornered and killed the pig. When Ralph tells them they let the fire go out, Jack sees the comment as irrelevant and continues relating what happened. As much as there is ecstasy, though, Jack still shows some twinges of repulsion, even as he laughs, although ultimately the killing is described as "a long satisfying drink."

Curiously, it is Ralph's voice that is described as "savage," since Ralph has been pushed to his limit by the hunters' irresponsibleness. He tells them loudly that they had seen a ship, and this finally silences the hunters. Jack tries to evade responsibility, and then when Ralph continues to press him and Piggy joins in, Jack says he needed as many people as he could get in the hunt, and once again the argument turns to the tasks of obtaining meat versus building shelters. Jack pushes his hair down on his forehead, exactly the opposite of Ralph, who had earlier been pushing his back. It is as if Jack is proclaiming that he likes the long, overgrown, savage hair. It emphasizes his savageness even further when, in the act of pushing the hair, he spreads blood, albeit unwittingly, from the hunted pig to his forehead.

When Piggy starts to chastise Jack again, some of the other hunters wail in agreement. Jack lashes out, punching Piggy in the stomach, and even after Ralph steps forward Jack smacks Piggy again, this time in the head, and forces his glasses to fly off. Simon rescues them, but now one side of the glasses is broken, weakening Piggy even further. Yet Piggy is not intimidated and threatens Jack, only to have Jack mimic him. This provokes the others to laugh, and even Ralph almost joins in but at the same time is angered at his own weakness.

Ralph chastises Jack again, and Jack finally apologizes, not for his treatment of Piggy but for letting the fire go out. He so clearly appears as a leader that Sam and Eric, who had been assigned responsibility for the fire, never appear guilty, as if Jack has such control over them that they had had to join him in the hunt. The hunters admire Jack for apologizing and wait to hear Ralph graciously accept, but he cannot. Instead Ralph tells them to light the fire, and all join in, relieved at some release of tension.

The fire cooks the pig for the whole group and brings them together, even Ralph and Piggy to some extent. When Ralph is given a piece of meat, he's described as chewing on it like a wolf, even though he would have liked to have turned it down. Indeed, this is another example of the wildness competing with the non-wild side, even within the chief himself. Jack makes a point of not giving any meat to Piggy, who asks disoriently where his is and gets an angry reply from Jack. Ralph feels uneasy, but Simon gives Piggy his meat, only to be laughed at by the twins and to then lower his face in shame. This angers Jack as well, who throws Simon another piece of meat and yells at him. Certainly Ralph must have realized that if he had given Piggy his meat, Jack would not have lashed out at him, yet Ralph hadn't moved and still doesn't say anything. Jack is raging and can only blurt short phrases. All are silent until Maurice asks about the hunt.

The hunters describe their experience and inspire the grinning twins to carry on and make pig-dying noises. Maurice then pretends to be the pig, and the hunters encircle him and pretend to beat him, dance, and sing their disturbing pig chant. Ralph has some mixed reactions and is described as "envious and resentful," but when they finally stop he says they will have an assembly at the platform immediately and leaves.

Chapter 5 opens with Ralph preparing for the meeting. While there have been several meetings already, this is the first time that we know of that Ralph spends any time preparing. He chooses to walk on the beach to think because it is the only place where one doesn't have to watch one's feet at every step. With this, Ralph realizes how exhausted he is from life on this island and recalls the first day when he explored with Simon and Jack, remembering it as if "it were part of a brighter childhood." There is a hopelessness and sadness in the comparison, for Ralph is still young but feels distanced from his own childhood, and whether he will be happy in the future seems unknown.

Ralph also realizes how "unpleasant" it is to be wearing a dirty shirt, ripped and uncomfortable shorts, and to have hair hanging in his eyes. As he approaches the platform, he sees how its triangular shape is not quite right and that the tipping log where many of the boys sit has never been fixed. His "strange mood of speculation that was so foreign to him" continues as he prepares to sound the conch shell. He sees that a chief must be wise and a good thinker but recognizes that he isn't a strong thinker, especially in comparison to Piggy. His values have shifted.

When all the boys are gathered, Ralph tries to explain things simply, so that even the smallest will understand. He explains that this is a serious assembly to set things straight and proceeds to describe what they're doing wrong, namely that decisions they make in meetings aren't carried out. They had decided, for example, to collect clear water and to keep it in a certain place, and to use one section of the rocks as a lavatory, yet these rules were only followed for a short while. Similarly, while many pitched in to build the first shelter, by the time they got to building the fourth, only Simon and himself completed the work.

As he speaks, Ralph is strong and steady, although at times the listening boys are giggling and not recognizing the seriousness of the situation. Ralph adds that without the fire they will die, but even this doesn't seem to focus their attention. With regard to the fire, he says that going forward they will only have a fire on the mountain. Many want to speak against this, but Ralph talks over the group and again tells them that they must listen to him since they named him chief.

Jack wants to interrupt, but Ralph says he still has more to say and then tells the group what they can talk about. He says that things started to go wrong when the boys began to get frightened, and he tells them they can work on "kind of deciding on the fear." Ralph again tells them, though, that there's nothing to their fear. But Jack takes a different tack. He's angry and calls the young boys names for being babies. He differentiates, too, between fear and the beast in the forest that many still believe is there. He says he has been over the whole island and no beast exists, so they shouldn't think about it. "And as for the fear—," he adds, "you'll have to put up with that like the rest of us." But there is no beast, he tells them again, and garners applause from the group.

Piggy speaks next, and even though he is made fun of, he persists and explains that not only is there no beast but there is no reason to be frightened. He purports that the world is scientific and that soon men will be traveling to Mars. He repeats that there is nothing to fear but then pauses and adds, "Unless we get frightened of people." When the others laugh and poke fun at this statement, Piggy turns to let the "littluns" speak, so, he says, the older boys can show them how silly they are. But when the first little one speaks and describes his terrifying experience, even though Ralph counters that the boy was having a nightmare at the time, the group sympathizes and is unsettled.

Piggy draws another small boy forward, whose behavior is quite similar to that of the first boy who spoke about a beast when they first started having meetings and then ended up lost and dying in the fire. Initially this next boy that Piggy cajoles will not speak, and Ralph and the others force him to do so. He provides his whole name, as well as his address and the beginning of his telephone number and breaks out weeping, at which point there are screams for him to be quiet, but he cannot stop. Other small boys start wailing as well, and the only thing that finally quiets them is when Maurice does some funny stunts.

Again the older boys dismiss the idea of the beast and press this small boy, Percival, to explain where this beast could possibly be hiding. He replies that it comes out of the sea, causing a new wave of fear among the group and explaining the chapter's title, "Beast from Water." Maurice becomes the first older boy to admit they don't know for sure that there isn't a beast, and this provokes complete chaos. Simon is the next oldest boy not to dismiss the beast completely. Again many are yelling as Simon asserts that the beast may only be "us." Simon tries vainly to explain "mankind's essential illness," after which someone suggests that maybe Simon is really speaking of a kind of ghost. With this, both Piggy and Jack want to speak and end up fighting for the conch shell until Ralph breaks in.

Ralph admits that he made a mistake by having the meeting so late, that perhaps this is not the topic to be discussing as it gets darker. While earlier he had shown growth by realizing Piggy's intellectual abilities, at this meeting he appears to have diminished in his role as leader. While he recognized the need for the meeting and started it off well, the topic of the beast was one that had been discussed previously and had not been effectively resolved then. Bringing up the beast again shows Ralph's seemingly irrational belief in the power of common sense to always triumph. To make matters worse, he asks for a vote to show if they believe in ghosts, even though, again, he probably will be unable to dissuade any believers.

In an attempt to save Ralph and the situation, Piggy berates the group: "What are we? Humans? Or animals? Or savages?

What's grownups going to think? Going off—hunting pigs—letting fires out—and now!" Jack shouts at Piggy to shut up, and when Ralph finally without prodding stands up for Piggy, Jack loses control. He tells Ralph to shut up and questions why he should be chief, since he gives orders that don't make sense, since he can't hunt or sing, and since he always favors Piggy. Ralph screams back that Jack's breaking the rules, "the only thing we've got!" But Jack says he doesn't care about the rules, gives a wild scream, and jumps off the platform. The participants disperse, screaming and laughing, and then chant in a revolving dancing mass.

Piggy and Ralph remain on the platform. Piggy urges him to sound the conch, but Ralph says if he does and the others do not come they will have lost everything—the fire won't be kept and there will be no rescue. "We'll be like animals," he says. Still Ralph puts the shell by his lips but then lowers it. He asks Piggy if there are ghosts and says he shouldn't be chief after all. Piggy tries to reassure him, and then they realize that someone else is sitting with them as well—Simon, who also says Ralph must remain chief.

Piggy wonders what would happen to him if Ralph weren't chief. Ralph, again unaware, says nothing would happen to him, but Piggy explains that Jack hates Ralph and Piggy, and since he can't fight Ralph, given the opportunity he'll fight Piggy. Simon concurs. Ralph says they're all drifting, and even this language indicates he doesn't see the enormity of the predicament, which is worse than just the boys drifting into chaos. The boys voice their wishes that a parent or caretaker were there, since then everything would be all right. As much as Piggy and Simon are keen observers, they still hold childish views of adults, believing adults always know what to do and never would have disintegrated like the children on the island have. Ralph seemingly foolishly wishes that the adults could give them some sign. The three are now so disturbed themselves that they jump to grab each other when they hear a chilling noise from the dark. The wail comes from Percival, although the three boys do not at first know what the sound is. Percival, this boy that no one wants to believe, is the last voice in the chapter, instilling fear among the strongest boys and a great foreboding.

The beast, the fear of which was first mentioned early in the book but has caused a commotion again, will remain the focus of the next chapter, **chapter 6**, since its title is "Beast from Air." The chapter is a direct continuation of the last. The boys settle Percival in a shelter, retire themselves, and finally fall asleep. While doing so, they are unaware of the battle being fought ten miles up over their heads. Ironically, the boys get the sign Ralph had requested but completely miss it. Unnoticed by them, an explosion occurs in the air and from it drops a person dangling in a parachute. This parachute eventually gets caught among the rocks of the mountaintop, hanging buy its lines and blown by the wind so that its body rocks back and forth depending on the gust.

Unaware of this occurrence as well are the twins, Sam and Eric, once again responsible for the fire on the mountaintop but not doing their job, since they are both asleep and the fire is nearly out. When they wake up, they are relieved that they can get it started again and laugh at the thought of how angry Ralph would have been if he had seen what had happened. Only fifteen yards away from them is the tangled parachutist, whose parachute is making noise as it's blown open. When the two hear its noise and see a dark humped figure, they scramble down the mountain mad with fear.

Ralph is having pleasant dreams, but the terrified twins interrupt his sleep. They tell him they saw the beast. Ralph calls to Piggy for the spears, and they dare not venture out but wait until morning and hold a meeting. The twins describe the beast as furry, with wings, teeth, and claws and say that it followed them down from the mountain, slinking behind trees. All are horrified. Jack asks who is ready to hunt the creature, but Ralph hesitates, wondering what they can do with meager wooden spears, who will take care of the small boys if the others leave, and how they can find a beast that leaves no tracks.

Ralph says Piggy will stay with the small boys; Jack charges that this is favoritism once again. Piggy is anxious about being left behind, and Jack berates him, quite angry now. When Piggy says he has the conch and therefore the right to speak, Jack says the rules about speaking are unnecessary, that there are only a few people that should be speaking and making decisions. The battle continues when Ralph fumes and tells Jack to sit down but Jack won't. He can't wait to go, saying this is a hunter's job, but Ralph reminds him again that there are no tracks and that they also have to relight the fire that must have gone out by now. The boys are all on Ralph's side now.

Ralph asks Jack what area he hasn't patrolled on the island yet, and decides that's where they will go to search, at the very end where the great rocks are. At Ralph's direction, all the older boys eat first rather than just setting out, and then Ralph decides that Jack can lead. Simon is just in front of Ralph and doubts the existence of the beast, although he doesn't voice this to the others. It makes no sense, he thinks, that a beast with claws that scratched would leave no tracks and would not be fast enough to catch the twins. Golding tells us, "However Simon thought of the beast, there rose before his inward sight the picture of a human at once heroic and sick." Now we see that Simon has an ability the others don't, to see or know what we assume is probably the truth without literally seeing it. In this case, it makes sense that the parachutist was heroic and now is possibly sick. After contemplating his vision, Simon becomes perturbed at his inability to speak in front of the others. Then, as he slows down to walk next to Ralph and is pleased to see him smile at him, Simon bashes into a tree, again belittled and a comic figure rather than one with an important message.

When they arrive at the end of the island near the bottom of the rocky cliff, Ralph realizes he must go forward since he is the chief. As he hesitates and asks if this really is the logical place to go, Simon voices his disbelief that a beast exists, but none take it seriously. Ralph makes it to the narrow neck of rock and looks to the other side of the island, quite frightened to see the massive swell of the Pacific that "seemed like the breathing of some stupendous creature." This is the first clue we have of the geographic location of the island, and we realize that the boys are indeed very far from home.

Jack then catches up to Ralph, not comfortable letting him go on his own. They make it to the last peak, and Jack starts to ask Ralph if he remembers the first day when they had explored there, but his sentence is broken off with the realization of all the negative things that have happened between them. Jack looks at the huge rock there and thinks of how great it would be to heave it down on an enemy. But Ralph looks over toward the mountain where their fire should be and is disturbed by its nonexistence once again. He decides they must go back and climb the mountain, since this is where the twins saw the beast and they need to start the fire.

Ralph is intent on getting up the mountain, but when the others realize Ralph and Jack have found no beast they start to play and roll rocks. As Ralph tries to make his point clear, though, there is a sentence that reminds us of what Simon has just gone through. Golding writes: "A strange thing happened in his [Ralph's] head. Something flittered there in front of his mind like a bat's wing, obscuring his idea." It is as if there is a vision for Ralph to see but he as yet hasn't the capacity to grasp it. He tells the boys they're wasting their time when they need a fire and they argue with him and plead that he not push them immediately into this next mission. Angry, Ralph hits his knuckles against a rock as he's done before on this trip but this time it doesn't seem to hurt; he, like Simon, stands out from the others. He berates the boys again, and they go silent, "mutinously."

Chapter 7 is a direct continuation of the action from chapter 6, again indicating an urgency and adding to the tension of searching for the beast. There is an ominousness in its title, "Shadows and Tall Trees," yet a certain relief in it, since, unlike the two previous chapter titles, this one doesn't include the word "beast."

The boys are continuing along the rocks to get to the mountaintop. They stop to eat some fruit, and Ralph realizes how hot it is and how good it would be to wash his stiff shirt, cut his hair, bathe with soap, and brush his teeth. On this side of the island, flanked by the vast roaring sea instead of the calm lagoon, "one was helpless, one was condemned, one was—."

Ralph doesn't finish his thought, but the brutishness of nature on this side of the island only reinforces the boys' fear and the breaking down of their community. Ralph's thoughts are interrupted when Simon tells him that he will make it home. Ralph, more the pragmatist and also perhaps struck by the strength of Simon's assertion, asks him how he "knows" this. Simon is content to explain that he just thinks it, but Ralph calls him "batty." Still the two end up smiling at each other, apparently each accepting the other and perhaps thankful to be focusing, even for a moment, on a dream.

Roger sees signs of pigs, and Ralph agrees that they can hunt them, as long as doing so will take them in the right direction. Now a tense group of hunters, the boys move forward more slowly, and when they have to stop for a moment, Ralph daydreams of his life at home. He, like Piggy, actually, had not had it too easy, since he had lived in several homes and his mother had not always been with the family, but still the daydream is rather idyllic and the longest in the book. It contrasts with the harsh surroundings and the tension of the hunt, making the boys' current situation appear even bleaker.

The daydream is interrupted by mayhem in the pig track, and Ralph sees the others scramble and then a boar storming directly toward him. He throws his sharpened stick, lodging it in the animal's snout. Jack orders the group in the chase, but the boar gets away.

Despite the overall defeat, Ralph himself feels victorious for having inflicted the wound. He's excited, asks the others to confirm that they saw it, "sunned himself in their new respect and felt that hunting was good after all." Jack is angry that Ralph threw at the wrong time, and when he shows that he's bloody from the boar's tusks, attention shifts to him.

Ralph, not to be deterred, explains how he threw at the boar, and Robert snarls at him, pretends he's the pig, and the others join in jabbing him. Jack, again in charge, hollers for them to make a ring, and they encircle Robert, who's still pretending but then is in real pain and calls out for them to stop. Jack holds him by the hair and is ready with his knife; the others join in their chant: "Kill the pig! Cut his throat! Kill the pig! Bash him in!" Ralph, too, is jabbing and fights to get closer. His "desire to squeeze and hurt was over-mastering," Golding writes.

When Jack signals, the boys stop and the group collapses, dreaming up what they can do next time to improve what Jack calls "the game." Robert, even though he has just been the victim, says they need a real pig, since they've got to kill it. The suggestions end with Jack's idea that they could just use a "littlun." Everyone laughs, and this only increases the intensely chilling scene.

Now Ralph takes charge, saying they must move on. Maurice and the twins suggest that they wait until the morning to climb the mountain, but Ralph and Jack persist. The path is tougher now, rocky, with little cliffs, and eventually they are confronted with an impossible cliff. Ralph says someone must go back to Piggy to let him know they will be gone until after dark. Jack makes fun of the chief for once again worrying about Piggy. Simon volunteers and heads off, while Ralph, infuriated at Jack, questions him about the island terrain so he can decide on a new path. But he realizes it's getting dark and wonders if they should continue, only to be taunted again by Jack. Exasperated and remembering Piggy's earlier comment, Ralph asks Jack directly, "Why do you hate me?" The only response is a stirring among the others.

Ralph leads the way, through a pig-track, until it opens and they see the stars in the sky. He says they will cut across, go back to the others, and climb the next day. The others agree, except for Jack, who mocks Ralph for his cowardliness. Angered, Ralph decides he will climb, then says one more must come, in case they find anything. Roger volunteers, and they set off. They are surrounded by darkness and choke when they get near the ashes from the fire. Ralph realizes how foolish they are, and when Jack says he will go on by himself Ralph finally decides to let him.

It doesn't take long for Jack to make it back. Shivering and with a voice that's hardly recognizable as his own, he tells the other two he's seen a thing bulging on top, at which Ralph decides they will all go back up. Squeezed together, whispering, creeping on hands and knees, they go back and see the rock-like hump that looks something like a great ape that lifts its head in the wind to show a ruined face. The three boys rush away in terror.

Chapter 8 opens at dawn the next day. Ralph, Jack, and Piggy are together. Ralph says they could never fight the beast and ignores Jack when he offers for his hunters to take it on. Ralph adds a new twist—that since the thing is sitting right by their fire site, it must not want them to be rescued, and, indeed, they cannot have a fire. When Jack asks again whether his hunters can fight it, Ralph answers that they are only boys with sticks, maddening Jack who walks away.

The boys hear the conch, but this time Jack is the one blowing it. Rather than seeing this as a fight for power, Ralph walks to the platform for the meeting and takes the shell from Jack. The two argue over who is running the meeting, until Ralph just gives in. Jack says that they all know that the three boys have seen the beast. With this, the gathered boys express their fears again about it coming from the sea or even from the trees, and that it's hunting. Jack agrees that it's a hunter and tells them that it can't be killed.

But from here, Jack turns the meeting a new way—against Ralph. He says that Ralph has called his hunters no good, that Ralph thinks they are cowards. He says Ralph is the real coward, though, that he's not a hunter, that unlike Jack he's not a prefect (a student who has been given some disciplinary authority over others). With each point, Ralph interrupts to stand up for himself and set the record straight. Finally Jack asks who in the group thinks Ralph should no longer be chief. But the response is only silence. Destroyed, Jack puts down the shell, and as tears run down his face he says he's "not going to play any longer. Not with you." He says he is going off by himself but that anyone who wants to hunt with him when he goes can do so. Ralph shouts after him as he takes off, but Jack yells back, enraged as the tears stream down. Ralph tells himself that Jack will come back, again not understanding the gravity of the situation.

Piggy starts to speak to the group, saying they don't need Jack Merridew and must make their own plans. He too doesn't realize the damage caused by Jack's leaving. Simon interrupts, and despite jeers from the group, says they should go up the mountain. When Piggy asks what is the point after the others had no success doing so, Simon whispers, "What else is there to do?" With another of his ideas dismissed, Simon then moves far away from the group.

Piggy, still supporting Ralph, says he knows Ralph is thinking that they must build a fire for a chance to be rescued. When Ralph disagrees, saying it's not possible to have a fire by the thing, Piggy says they will just have to create a fire at the base of the island. The boys set to work, and Piggy himself starts the fire with his one remaining lens. The "littluns" dance and sing as the flame grows, and there is a party-like atmosphere. Ralph and Piggy talk about the type and size of the fire they should keep as well as maintaining a schedule for taking care of it. As the "littluns" drift away, Ralph realizes how few older boys are left, and the more observant Piggy says he saw some of them go off in Jack's direction. To help rally their spirits, Piggy leaves with Sam and Eric and they return and surprise Ralph with ripe fruit so they can have their own feast. Ralph, apparently getting better at being more conscious of others' activities, asks if Simon has left to climb the mountain, but Piggy only laughs, calling Simon cracked.

Simon has actually gone to his quiet spot hidden in the brush, where he kneels down and then sits, despite the heat. One wonders if he has gone here to prepare himself to climb the mountain, to decide if he should, or to just be alone.

Much further down the beach, Jack now has his own small group of followers, the choir boys who have again donned their weathered black caps. He tells them he is the chief, that they will hunt and not concern themselves over the beast. Curiously, he adds, "We shan't dream so much down here. This is near the end of the island." When he says they won't dream so much, perhaps he means like the small boys who are babies for crying in their sleep, or like Ralph and Piggy who he may believe do too much thinking. The comment about their location indicates that they are far from the others and at the same time near the end, a more precarious spot and one also connoting that there is not much further to go. In a more general way, it could also indicate that their time on the island is limited, its own end having arrived.

Jack also says he will get more of the older boys to join them, they will hunt a pig, have a feast, and leave some for the beast in the hopes that it will keep him from chasing them. They leave for the hunt immediately, and Jack quickly finds a group of unsuspecting pigs lounging in the shade. Making blatant his wickedness and lack of compassion, he intends to chase the sow that is resting with her piglets. Jack gives the order, and they aim and then throw their spears, which now have fire-hardened points. They race after the pig, who almost loses them at first, but since Jack is more experienced at hunting, he finds her trail. They follow her as the afternoon goes on, "wedded to her in lust, excited by the long chase and the dropped blood." Finally they can move in, and Jack and Roger do the last stabs, with Jack cutting her throat. Blood spouts, Jack laughs, and when he shows the boys his bloody palms, they laugh too.

Jack says he will invite the others to a feast, but Roger asks how he can do so since they don't have a fire. "We'll raid them," Jack says, not for a moment thinking there could be any more logical, peaceful way. But before he can leave, they must make an offering to the beast, and Jack cuts off the pig's head and mounts it on a stick, near the pig's guts that have already attracted flies. He calls the head a gift, which explains the chapter's title, "Gift for the Darkness." All had stepped back when he mounted the head, and now all run away as fast as possible.

The narrative turns back to Simon, who, we now realize, has remained hidden and is actually not so far from the skewered sow's head. Her half-shut eyes are described as "dim with the infinite cynicism of adult life. They assured Simon that everything was a bad business." Simon says that he knows this, apparently feeling as if the head is speaking to him. The head is repeatedly described as grinning and dripping. It sneers negativity and seemingly cannot be pushed aside, since even as it drips, dismembered and dead, it still ominously communicates. The monstrosity is called the Lord of the Flies, a translation of "Beelzebub," which also is the name for the devil, the ultimate evil.

The scene shifts to Ralph and Piggy lying in the sand by the fire, as dark clouds and thunder that sounds like a gun are portentously heard overhead. Ralph admits to Piggy that he's scared, that he doesn't understand why the others don't recognize the importance of the fire, and that sometimes even he doesn't care about it. He wonders what would happen if he got to be like the others. Piggy says they would just have to go on, since that's what adults would do. Now Ralph recognizes that he can slip like the others. He is awakening to the idea that Piggy and Simon have already both realized, that the main beast to be scared of is the others or even themselves. When Ralph asks what causes things to break apart, Piggy says he thinks it's Jack, and Ralph agrees; now they both recognize a source of evil that is separate from themselves.

At this moment, boys with painted faces burst from the forest, and everyone but Ralph flees. Two of the painted boys take branches from the fire and leave, while three remain, one being Jack, now completely naked except for a belt. Jack announces to all that his group is hunting, feasting, and having fun and that if the others want to join them they should let him know and he will decide if he will include them or not. He invites them to feast with his group that night and then before departing he shouts at the other two painted boys with him, who hesitate but then raise their spears and recite together, "The Chief has spoken." They leave.

Ralph and the others have a meeting. Ralph explains what happened but then forgets what else he wanted to say. With Piggy's help, he stumbles quite poorly through his remaining few words, reminding the boys that the fire is the most important thing, since it can bring about their rescue. Even the youngest listeners realize the weakness in his words. Plus, seriously missing from his talk is any clear plan or response to Jack being his own chief and looking for recruits.

Bill suggests that they go to the feast and tell the other group that keeping the fire going is too much for them. It's unclear if he thinks they should tell Jack's group that they need their help or if he thinks they should join Jack's group. He and the twins say it must be fun to hunt and be "savages." They are tempted by the meat. Ralph interrupts to ask why they can't get their own meat, and the others reply that they don't want to go into the jungle. Even Piggy is enticed by the meat, and the thunder sounds overhead once again, this time like a cannon.

We are returned to Simon and the Lord of the Flies. The head tells the boy that it is the beast and that it is a part of him as well. Now it speaks in the voice of a schoolmaster. It warns Simon that he is not wanted, that they will have fun on the island, and warns him that if he tries anything, the others, including Ralph and Piggy, will destroy him. With this, Simon falls unconscious.

Chapter 9 is entitled "A View to a Death," and is the only one with the word "Death" in it. The clouds are still building and "ready to explode." We read that the vessels in Simon's nose had broken, blood had poured out, and Simon fell asleep after his "fit." Now he wakes up and says, "What else is there to do?" This is the same question he posed at the meeting after the three boys had reported seeing the beast at the top of the mountain. Simon will climb the mountain by himself, despite being the physically weak boy who is ridiculed, who's too afraid to talk at meetings, and who has just been threatened by the Lord of the Flies. As he climbs, he staggers at times from being so tired, but he continues until he gets near the humped figure and then close enough to determine what it actually is. He gets sick from seeing the parachutist's decomposed body but then untangles the parachute lines and sets them loose. The figure sits beside him as Simon peers down to the boys, many if not all of whom appear to be further up the island's beach away from the platform. Then Simon starts down the mountain, still staggering, to let the others know the truth about the supposed beast.

Ralph and Piggy are still near their original camp, swimming. The first thing Ralph says is, "Bathing, that's the only thing to do." This line, similar to Simon's, points out a striking contrast. Simon is intent on doing something about the supposed beast at the top of the mountain, whereas Ralph is nearly at a loss over what they are to do and so utters his facetious line. Even though Ralph has come to recognize Piggy's value, he still teases him in the water here, but, for once, Piggy fights back and does so quite furiously. Ralph backs off and asks where everyone is, and once again Piggy is shown to be quite aware and says the others have gone to Jack's party. Ralph has been outdone by both Piggy and Simon.

Ralph and Piggy head toward the party as well and approach the laughing, singing, relaxing boys, most of whom are nearly done eating. Jack is sitting in the center on a great log; he still is painted and now also is garlanded "like an idol." Ralph and Piggy are given meat and stand off together, as Jack tells all to sit. He asks who wants to join his "tribe," but Ralph inserts that he is chief. The two spar verbally, although Ralph is weakened at a couple points. When some of the listening boys say they want to join Jack, Piggy leads Ralph away, warning that there's going to be trouble. Thunder sounds again, and now great raindrops begin to fall. Ralph reminds them that he has shelters but Jack doesn't. All are disturbed by the storm; some of the young boys run around and scream.

Jack yells for all to dance, and between bursts of lightning Roger takes the part of the pig, charging at Jack, as the others grab spears, cooking spits, and firewood weapons. Piggy and Ralph join in, "eager to take a place in this demented but partly secure society. They were glad to touch the brown backs of the fence that hemmed in the terror and made it governable." The group takes up the killing chant, and Roger moves out of the circle to become a hunter rather than the hunted.

Simon crawls out of the forest into the group of yelling boys and tries to scream over them about the dead parachutist. He breaks out of the circle, but the hunters chase after him and are out of control, forcing Simon into the role of beast. They "leapt on to the beast, screamed, struck, bit, tore. There were no words, and no movements but the tearing of teeth and claws." Great torrents of rain surge down. The struggling group on the sand breaks up, and the boys stagger away, leaving "the beast" there, unmoving, near the sea edge, where "already its blood was staining the sand."

Disturbed by the great storm, the parachutist falls from the mountain, alighting very near the boys, who scream and take off. The great parachute canvas and its dead passenger finally are blown out to sea.

Near midnight, the storm is gone, the sky and water are clear, and "strange, moonbeam-bodied creatures with fiery eyes" are near Simon's broken body. His head lit with brightness, his "cheek silvered" and the line of his shoulder "became sculptured marble." His body advances into the sea.

Golding has said that Simon is the Christ figure, misunderstood, laughed at, contemplative, solitary, who has a message but is killed. In Golding's book, though, the great message makes it to no one, and a new religion isn't created as a result of this life and death.

Chapter 10 again opens with Piggy and Ralph. Ralph, with a swollen cheek that's reduced his eye to a slit, and a scarred knee, limps toward Piggy, who's sitting on the platform, a place of democracy, order, and problem solving that now seems powerless. Piggy tells Ralph that the only ones left are some of the "littluns" and the twins, who are collecting wood. Ralph sits on the platform as well but faces the conch and the chief's seat rather than sitting in that designated spot. Ralph whispers something that Piggy can't hear, and then repeats, "Simon." Piggy just nods, and they stay silent again.

Ralph caresses the light gleaming conch and asks yet again what they are going to do. He laughs sharply at the thought of calling a meeting. When he stops, he speaks again of Simon, saying bluntly that they murdered him. However, no matter what Ralph says, Piggy tries to rationalize. He warns Ralph not to admit to the twins that they were a part of the dance. When the twins appear with wood for the fire, they say they got lost in the forest after the feast. Piggy says he and Ralph left early, and the twins say they did the same. Ralph is silent and lets the others weave their stories; all have been shaken by the experience, but there apparently can be no talking about it.

Meanwhile, Jack's group has its own reaction to the horrible events. Jack has started to get the boys to set up a protective cave at the place where the main island meets the jutting Castle Rock. He reminds the boys that the beast may try to break in, like it crawled in on them the other night in its disguise. A boy tries to clarify what happened, but Jack yells that they didn't kill the beast: "No! How could we—kill—it?" While it was disturbing to hear Piggy, the twins, and Ralph deny Simon's homicide, let alone partaking in it, in Jack's group the situation is much worse, for none mention Simon's name. Jack also continues to encourage ancient pagan ritual, reminding them they must leave a present for the beast after a hunt. Again one of the boys questions how they will make a fire, showing Jack again as remiss about a basic need.

At that moment, Ralph and the others are making a fire, although it is quite tough to do, since everything is still rather wet from the storm. They think about getting rescued, and Ralph thinks about the figure in the parachute; this is the first we're told that anyone had seen very much of the figure that had floated down by them. He says that Simon had been trying to tell them something about a dead man, but none of the others around Ralph seem to hear, and he himself doesn't seem to have pieced together the entire mystery.

Since the two are disheartened about tending the fire with so few boys left in their group and since the logs and other fuel are so wet, they decide to forget about the fire for the night and to start it again in the morning. They all turn in for the night, and Ralph dreams of being home but must alter the dream when he realizes that some of the places he had once considered so idyllic because they are naturally wild no longer have any appeal for him. He is awoken by Piggy, who says he's been making a disturbing noise, and the two see that the twins are fighting with each other in their sleep. It used to be that only the smallest ones suffered such disturbances.

Ralph again is woken by Piggy, who says he hears something. Ralph hears nothing at first but then does, and the two boys are greatly frightened. A horrid voice close by outside the shelter whispers for Piggy to come out. Ralph tells him not to answer, and as the voice calls again as Piggy has an asthma attack. Shortly the creatures outside invade the shelter, and a great brawl ensues in the darkness. When the shelter collapses there is more chaos, and the dark figures escape.

When the remaining boys pull themselves out and check on Piggy, they realize he is breathing somewhat better. All have been battered, and when they tell their own tales about what they did to the enemy, Ralph realizes they have, in fact, also fought each other in the confusion. Piggy says he thought they came for the conch shell, but when Ralph checks its glimmering whiteness is still sitting by the platform, ready for another meeting to help bring about some structure and order. Piggy knows what they really wanted though, since his glasses are missing. Without them he cannot see, and now he turns to Ralph and asks a question similar to the one that Ralph has recently been asking Piggy: "[W]hat am I going to do?" The chapter's title is "The Shell and the Glasses." They are two of the most important tools on the island, but while losing the shell would be a disturbing event for Ralph's group, the loss of the glasses means they lose their mechanism for starting a fire—their only hope for rescue—and that Piggy becomes notably weakened.

The boys who have taken the glasses are returning to their camp, turning cartwheels as they go. This immediately draws to mind the image of Ralph who very early in the book had taken such delight in the island's riches and its lack of adults that he would stand on his head. These cartwheeling boys, however, are delighting in having power over the others. We assume, also, since Jack never felt that keeping a fire was a priority that by his gaining the glasses the chance of getting rescued drops significantly.

In **chapter 11** Ralph blows on ashes to see if there might still be enough spark to start a new fire, but there is none. At Piggy's prompting, Ralph calls an assembly and then pushes Piggy to speak first. Piggy says they must figure out a way to get his glasses back, that Ralph is the only one on the island who's accomplished anything and that he must tell them what to do. Ralph reminds the group of how Jack had let the fire go out before, just when a ship had been passing. He alludes to Simon's death being Jack's fault as well. When pressed for a plan, Ralph says they should clean themselves up like they used to be to show they aren't savages and then approach the other group. The twins agree but undermine with the non-savage concept by saying they will bring swords as well.

Piggy asks what grown-ups will think of the events on the island. This demonstrates he believes they will be rescued some day and also shows his lack of understanding that they are trapped on the island because of the violence of adults. He is bolder than Ralph here, since he calls Simon's death murder, and he mentions the young boy who died in the fire when they first arrived on the island. He says he will go to Jack Merridew with the conch in his hand. He recites what he'll say, explaining that he will tell Jack he must give his glasses back because it's the right thing to do. He is trembling and tears fall from his eyes. We realize that his logic will not work on Jack and that his own fear will make the confrontation impossible. But Ralph says Piggy can try his plan and that he and the twins will go with him.

The meeting is dismissed, so the four boys can eat and prepare to leave. Again Ralph says the boys should "be like we were," and wash and possibly comb their hair. But the boys have other ideas, and Ralph gives in, realizing that it is impossible to look the way he would like them to and possibly realizing as well that no matter how they look, they cannot go back to the way they were. Again the twins are off track and suggest that maybe they should paint their faces. But Ralph is adamantly against this and yells that they will not do it. Then he must fight to remember what is important—the smoke that can get them rescued. This lack of memory shows that he is weakened mentally as well as physically. Piggy chimes in, and Ralph berates him, angry that Piggy is finishing his thoughts as if he cannot remember himself, which does seem to be the case. The twins look more closely at Ralph.

The four set off, with Ralph limping along first, visually impared because of the hot haze, his long hair, and his swollen face that presses his eye partially closed. He seems unaware that there is great potential for something horrible to happen. The boys seem to instinctively know that the others will be at

Castle Rock (the title of the chapter), that neck of land, with a ledge surrounding its rock, and red rock pinnacles far above. As they head out on the neck, they are forty feet above the water, and Piggy questions the safety of the situation.

From the pinnacle comes a fake war cry and someone shouts down to ask who they are. Ralph sees Roger way above him and shouts back that he can see who they are and therefore is "silly" for asking. Ralph blows the conch shell and says he is calling an assembly. The "savages" guarding the neck don't move. They snicker slightly, and Ralph repeats that he is calling an assembly. Finally Ralph asks where Jack is. They tell him he is hunting and has ordered that no one be allowed in. Ralph explains why he and the others have come, and again there is laughter.

Jack, back from his hunt, comes up behind Ralph and asks what he wants. Piggy cries out in fear, and the boys on the rock jeer loudly. Ralph says Jack must return Piggy's glasses, that it was a "dirty trick" to have stolen the glasses like a thief, and that they would have given Jack fire if he had only asked for it.

Jack rushes at Ralph to stab his chest, but Ralph blocks it. After additional strikes, there is an unstated mutual agreement to not use the spears for stabbing. Breathing heavily, the boys now part and taunt each other. Even in his vulnerable state, Piggy reminds Ralph that their goal is to get the glasses and be able to restart their fire. Ralph realizes that he is right, relaxes his tight muscles, and rests his spear butt on the ground. He restates that they've come for the glasses, and again Piggy must whisper to him that they are important because of the fire. Reminded, Ralph tells the others of the fire's importance, but they laugh and make him more angry. Calling them "painted fools," Ralph says that he and Piggy and the twins are not enough to keep the fire going. There is silence now.

The direct, logical approach fails, however, as we expect. Jack orders his men to grab the twins and tie them up. While at first they hesitate, they then do as commanded and feel powerful. Jack, as would be expected of a devil, attempts a blow at Ralph from behind, but Ralph fends it off. Now Ralph loses his temper and screams that Jack is "a beast and a swine and a bloody, bloody thief!" Calling Jack a beast is most fitting, since the beast has come to symbolize evil and has provoked great fear. Calling him a swine works to demean him to a helpless, hunted animal and forces him out of the role of powerful hunter. Calling him a "bloody, bloody thief" is appropriate because of his burglary not only of the glasses but of the boys' goodness. While "bloody" is used in England as a curse or for emphasis, it also is significant here since Jack is happy to kill pigs and also was partly responsible for Simon's death—both instances involving blood.

Ralph charges at Jack, and Jack rushes toward Ralph as well. Now they use fists and hear the "shrill cheering of the tribe." Again, Piggy interrupts. He shouts that he has the conch, the boys fall silent, showing the power of the symbol even in the worst circumstance. In the silence, Ralph hears a stone fall past his head; Roger has thrown it, while his other hand is on the lever under a huge rock. Piggy yells at them for "acting like a crowd of kids," which, of course, is ironic, since this is what they are. When they boo, he still can silence them by holding up the shell. He offers them alternatives—between being a "pack of Indians" or being sensible like Ralph, and then between having rules and agreeing or hunting and killing. Ralph adds to the choices as well, but then Jack starts yelling. Jack has now backed into the spear-yielding tribe, and they appear ready to charge.

Ralph and Piggy seem minute against the throng. "The storm of sound beat at them," Golding writes, "an incantation of hatred. High overhead, Roger, with a sense of delirious abandonment, leaned all his weight on the lever." Ralph hears the boulder coming and flings himself down. Yet Piggy is hit. The conch shell explodes into pieces, and Piggy is hurled down the forty-foot drop. When he lands, his skull opens and releases "something," which we assume is his brain, seemingly the essential part of the intelligent boy's self and the part that has repeatedly helped the others as well. His body is immediately sucked into the sea.

All are silent, except Jack. He screams wildly and takes credit for the horrific death, warning Ralph that he will get the same treatment. He hollers that Ralph no longer has a tribe or a conch and that Jack is chief. Still, it is not enough that Ralph has seemingly lost everything. Jack wants him dead. He launches his spear at Ralph, and it tears by his ribs. The screaming tribe moves forward; two more spears fly by Ralph, and he runs, making it into the dense forest. Jack, the new chief, screams for all to head back to the fort. Then he turns to the twins and tells them they must join the tribe. He pokes Sam with a spear repeatedly, and then Roger comes to take over.

Chapter 12, the last in the book, is called "Cry of the Hunters" and, unlike many of the other chapter titles, we don't have to read through a good portion of the chapter before we understand its significance, although it gains additional significance at the very end of the book. When the chapter opens, Ralph is hiding but is still relatively close to Castle Rock, and as it gets darker he sneaks out of the ferns. Now he smells the roasting pig and realizes that while the others are feasting he will be safe. He toys with the notion that perhaps the tribe will actually leave him alone for the rest of their time on the island, but when he thinks about Simon and Piggy and Jack's hatred of him, he realizes the "savages" will come after him. He goes to find fruit to eat and then works his way back toward the rock at the end of the island.

Along the way, he encounters the pig's skull that "grinned" on the stick and "seemed to jeer at him cynically." Filled with anger and fear, Ralph strikes at it until it finally breaks and falls into two pieces, with its grin now notably wider as a result. He takes the spear that had been holding it up and backs away as he keeps his eyes on it. He appears more naïve than Simon, who while fearful of the head recognized its message of evil and that it could not be destroyed.

As Ralph gets closer to Castle Rock, he hears the boys' hunting chant. He discerns the figures of the twins in the sentry post, and it is a great blow to see them as part of this ghastly tribe. But not to be defeated, Ralph moves in and calls to them. When they realize it is Ralph, they tell him he must leave and even fiercely wave a spear.

Finally the twins tell Ralph that they were wounded and forced to be part of the tribe, and that Roger and "the chief" hate Ralph and are going "to do" him. All will hunt him tomorrow, and they explain that they will use signals as they search the island, spread out in a great line across it. Ralph asks what will happen if he's found and he gets no direct answer, as he hangs over the very rock far below where Piggy crashed. The twins warn him about Jack and Roger, and when they hear someone coming they fear that it is Roger himself checking to be sure they're doing their job. Quickly they throw Ralph a piece of meat. As he finds a place to hide in the ferns and grass, he hears Sam and Eric yelling on the top of the rock, panicked and in pain.

In the morning a hunter's cry wakes Ralph, and he crawls deep into the ferns and thicket, on the way glimpsing the legs of a "savage" coming toward him. The boy beats the ferns around Ralph but continues on, giving a signal cry to the others near him. For some time Ralph hears no more cries. He realizes as he looks around that the great rock that had sent Piggy to his death is actually now helping him, since it has created a great secure space.

Some time goes by, and then Ralph hears Roger and Jack ask one of the boys, "Are you certain?" Roger threatens the boy and hits him, and Ralph assumes the victim is one of the twins. Roger and Jack ask if this is where Ralph said he would hide, and this time a voice answers with a definite yes. Ralph tenses but then realizes he still is safe in the thick growth, that even if someone wormed his way in Ralph would have the advantage.

From the top of the rock, Ralph hears Jack's voice and then soon after hears the sound of a rock thundering down from the cliff. The thicket area is hit, but only broken twigs and leaves fall on Ralph. The boys cheer. Now Ralph fears the consequences as he hears the boys straining to push another enormous rock. Once released, its great force shoots Ralph into the air, and only a few feet from him the soil is wrenched up along with thicket, roots, stumps, and sticks.

Only shortly after this, Ralph hears whispering very close by. There is snickering, an objection, more snickering, and then, after the voices are gone, smoke appears. Ralph runs. He tries to decide on his best alternatives and repeatedly wishes he had time to think. He thinks he can either climb a tree or run through the line of boys and then run back, losing them. He's seen pigs get away like this, he thinks, and the thought only emphasizes his persistent optimism as well as his near helplessness, for while the plan can work, there also have been pigs that have been killed and Jack is much more of an expert hunter.

Ralph sees his third option as hiding. He hears a hunter's cry close to him, gets up from his temporary resting spot, and takes off again. By mistake he runs into the open and is directly in front of the broken pig skull that he had knocked off its skewer and broken. It still lies in the sand "jeering" and its enormous grin is a dreadful reminder that evil persists and may ultimately triumph.

Now out of the brambles and trees, Ralph sees more smoke and realizes the fire the boys have created is huge. He decides his best strategy is to hide, and after some searching he finds the hidden spot where Simon had so often retreated and never been found. For the reader, this brings to mind the fact that Simon told Ralph he thought Ralph would be saved; in addition, since we know that Golding has called Simon the Christ figure, we wonder if Ralph may be safe in this retreat, as if he is under Simon's care.

Ralph can hear the fire getting closer; the fruit trees, their primary food source, will soon be destroyed, and as animals run from the heat and smoke one wonders how many pigs may die as well. Now a hunter is quite near Ralph. Ralph readies himself with his spear, which he realizes is sharpened at both ends just like Roger's, showing there is no escaping the island savagery. The hunter comes closer, finds Ralph's hidden spot, but at first is unable to see clearly inside. Ralph sees that the boy is ready to poke in his spear, and Ralph shoots out with a burst of fear, strength, and anger. He pushes the boy over, but others are already moving in. He races from them and the rushing fire, stumbles, and right before he falls, sees a shelter erupt in flames; the shelters were one of the few symbols of civilization they had on the island and which he was largely responsible for building. Thrown to the ground, Ralph rolls over and over in the sand at the water's edge.

As he forces himself to his feet, he looks up into a huge peaked cap. We assume it is worn by one of the choir boys, since they are the only ones on the island that have caps. In the next sentence we are told the cap's peak is white, but we know the choir boys' hats are black. We read on and are given a description of the rest of the cap as well as of a uniform and gun. Again, like the shelter, these are symbols of civilization, although the gun reminds us that even in a civilized sphere, a weapon is needed. Finally, after the description of these items, we read that the person wearing them is a naval officer, who is accompanied by others in boats behind him. Ralph responds to him shyly, and the officer "inspected the little scarecrow....The kid," he thinks, "needed a bath, a haircut, a nose-wipe and a good deal of ointment." Immediately, then, we see Ralph not as the chief but as a little boy again.

The officer "grinned cheerfully," and says they saw the smoke coming from the island. Smoke, what Ralph has been continually telling the others was imperative for their rescue, does in fact bring it about, yet, ironically, this smoke has been created by Jack in an act of reckless, horrid aggression. The officer jokingly asks Ralph if they were having a war, and when Ralph nods affirmatively the officer, still believing the boys were playing, asks, "Nobody killed, I hope? Any dead bodies?" When Ralph tells him two are dead, the officer looks at him carefully, asks him the question again, and then realizes this is the truth.

"[T]he whole island was shuddering with flame," Golding writes. Only moments before, the palms at the platform, yet another symbol of order, were engulfed. More boys appear on the shore, and when the officer asks who the boss is, Ralph loudly says that he is, while behind him, Golding writes, another "little boy" with red hair almost announces that he is. The officer says that since the boys are all British, he would have expected that they "would have been able to put up a better show." Again, there is still the language of make-believe being used here, as if the boys had not been trying to get by and live but had been playing or acting; this seems somewhat appropriate, though, since in some way their experience on the island has seemed an unreal experience.

The officer is ready to take the boys from the island, but his comment about how they behaved brings Ralph to tears. He cries and shakes with sobs, and others join in. "Ralph wept for the end of innocence, the darkness of man's heart, and the fall through the air of the true, wise friend called Piggy," Golding writes.

The book ends, some have criticized, with a gimmick that saves Ralph just in time. Yet the ending, however forced it may seem, does remind us that the evil that has taken place here has all been at the hands of little boys. Also, ironically, the boys are being rescued from this evil by an armed ship that will bring them back to civilization, which has been in the throws of its own horrid war.

Critical Views

WILLIAM GOLDING
ON THE WORK AS A FABLE

With all its drawbacks and difficulties, it was this method of presenting the truth as I saw it in fable form which I adopted for the first of my novels which ever got published. The overall intention may be stated simply enough. Before the second world war I believed in the perfectibility of social man; that a correct structure of society would produce goodwill; and that therefore you could remove all social ills by a reorganization of society. It is possible that today I believe something of the same again; but after the war I did not because I was unable to. I had discovered what one man could do to another. I am not talking of one man killing another with a gun, or dropping a bomb on him or blowing him up or torpedoing him. I am thinking of the vileness beyond all words that went on, year after year, in the totalitarian states. It is bad enough to say that so many Jews were exterminated in this way and that, so many people liquidated—lovely, elegant word—but there were things done during that period from which I still have to avert my mind less I should be physically sick. They were not done by the headhunters of New Guinea, or by some primitive tribe in the Amazon. They were done, skilfully, coldly, by educated men, doctors, lawyers, by men with a tradition of civilization behind them, to beings of their own kind. I do not want to elaborate this. I would like to pass on; but I must say that anyone who moved through those years without understanding that man produces evil as a bee produces honey, must have been blind or wrong in the head. Let me take a parallel from a social situation. We are commonly dressed, and commonly behave as if we had no genitalia. Taboos and prohibitions have grown up round that very necessary part of the human anatomy. But in sickness, the whole structure of man must be exhibited to the doctor. When the occasion is important enough, we admit to what we have. It seems to me that in nineteenth-century and early twentieth-century society of the West, similar taboos grew up round the nature of man. He was supposed not to have in him, the sad fact of his own cruelty and lust. When these capacities emerged into action they were thought aberrant. Social systems, political systems were composed, detached from the real nature of man. They were what one might call political symphonies. They would perfect most men, and at the least, reduce aberrance.

Why, then, have they never worked? How did the idealist concepts of primitive socialism turn at last into Stalinism? How could the political and philosophical idealism of Germany produce as its ultimate fruit, the rule of Adolf Hitler? My own conviction grew that what had happened was that men were putting the cart before the horse. They were looking at the system rather than the people. It seemed to me that man's capacity for greed, his innate cruelty and selfishness, was being hidden behind a kind of pair of political pants. I believed then, that man was sick—not exceptional man, but average man. I believed that the condition of man was to be a morally diseased creation and that the best job I could do at the time was to trace the connection between his diseased nature and the international mess he gets himself into.

To many of you, this will seem trite, obvious and familiar in theological terms. Man is a fallen being. He is gripped by original sin. His nature is sinful and his state perilous. I accept the theology and admit the triteness; but what is trite is true; and a truism can become more than a truism when it is a belief passionately held. I looked round me for some convenient form in which this thesis might be worked out, and found it in the play of children. I was well situated for this, since at this time I was teaching them. Moreover, I am a son, brother, and father. I have lived for many years with small boys, and understand and know them with awful precision. I decided to take the literary convention of boys on an island, only make them real boys instead of paper cutouts with no life in them; and try to show how the shape of the society they evolved would be conditioned by their diseased, their fallen nature.

(...)

Ballantyne's island was a nineteenth-century island inhabited by English boys; mine was to be a twentieth-century island inhabited by English boys. I can say here in America what I should not like to say at home; which is that I condemn and detest my country's faults precisely because I am so proud of her many virtues. One of our faults is to believe that evil is somewhere else and inherent in another nation. My book was to say you think that now the war is over and an evil thing destroyed, you are safe because you are naturally kind and decent. But I know why the thing rose in Germany. I know it could happen in any country. It could happen here.

E.M. Forster's Introduction to *Lord of the Flies*

It is possible to read the book at a political level, and to see in its tragic trend the tragedy of our inter-war world. There is no doubt as to whose side the author is on here. He is on Ralph's. But if one shifts the vision to a still deeper level—the psychological—he is on the side of Piggy. Piggy knows that things mayn't go well because he knows what boys are, and he knows that the island, for all its apparent friendliness, is equivocal.

The hideous accidents that promote the reversion to savagery fill most of the book, and the reader must be left to endure them—and also to embrace them, for somehow or other they are entangled with beauty. The greatness of the vision transcends what is visible. At the close, when the boys are duly rescued by the trim British cruiser, we find ourselves on their side. We have shared their experience and resent the smug cheeriness of their rescuers. The naval officer is a bit disappointed with what he finds—everyone filthy dirty, swollen bellies, faces daubed with clay, two missing at least and the island afire. It ought to have been more like Coral Island, he suggests.

Ralph looked at him dumbly. For a moment he had a fleeting picture of the strange glamour that had once invested the beaches. But the island was scorched up like dead wood—Simon was dead—and Jack had ... The tears began to flow and sobs shook him. He gave himself up to them now for the first time on the island; great, shuddering spasms of grief that seemed to wrench his whole body. His voice rose under the black smoke before the burning wreckage of the island; and infected by that emotion, the other little boys began to shake and sob too. And in the middle of them, with filthy body, matted hair, and unwiped nose, Ralph wept for the end of innocence, the darkness of man's heart, and the fall through the air of the true, wise friend called Piggy.

This passage—so pathetic—is also revealing. Phrases like "the end of innocence" and "the darkness of man's heart" show us the author's attitude more clearly than has appeared hitherto. He believes in the Fall of Man and perhaps in Original Sin. Or if he does not exactly believe, he fears; the same fear infects his second novel, a difficult and profound work called *The Inheritors*. Here the innocent (the boys as it were) are Neanderthal Man, and the corrupters are Homo Sapiens, our own ancestors, who eat other animals, discover intoxicants, and destroy. Similar notions occur in his other novels.

Thus his attitude approaches the Christian: we are all born in sin, or will all lapse into it. But he does not complete the Christian attitude, for the reason that he never introduces the idea of a Redeemer. When a deity does appear, he is the Lord of the Flies, Beelzebub, and he sends a messenger to prepare his way before him.

(...)

Lord of the Flies is a very serious book which has to be introduced seriously. The danger of such an introduction is that it may suggest that the book is stodgy. It is not. It is written with taste and liveliness, the talk is natural, the descriptions of scenery enchanting. It is certainly not a comforting book. But it may help a few grownups to be less complacent and more compassionate, to support Ralph, respect Piggy, control Jack, and lighten a little the darkness of man's heart. At the present moment (if I may speak personally) it is respect for Piggy that seems needed most. I do not find it in our leaders.

FREDERICK R. KARL ON THE METAPHYSICAL NOVELS OF WILLIAM GOLDING

As in Greene's novels, there are beliefs and values operating in Golding's fiction that must dominate despite the main thrust of each novel toward disbelief. For most of his narrative, he seems to be concerned with moral aimlessness: the stranded boys in *Lord of the Flies*, for example, almost entirely shake off their civilized behavior. Under certain conditions of survival, the primitive element predominates; residual savagery lies barely below the surface and is controlled only under the right circumstances. Remove these circumstances and the boys are amoral, vicious, chaotic, murderous. What Golding senses is that institutions and order imposed from without are temporary, but that man's irrationality and urge for destruction are enduring.

The stranded boys under Ralph's leadership divide into two groups, those who will supply the food and those who will keep the fire, their only hope of attracting attention. In a way, the fire-keepers are the poets, the contemplative ones, while the hunters are the doers, the men of action. As in the real world, so here, the hunters begin to woo the fire-keepers, for to do is more glamorous than to be. Having first aimed at their common salvation, the two groups soon divide into warring factions. Ralph, however, possesses the conch shell (a symbol of his "poetic" power), which attracts some of the boys to his side, but even that piece of magic is eventually destroyed when the hunters become violent. Physical, force comes to smother magic, religion, creativity, humanity itself.

(...)

When the boys on the island struggle for supremacy, they reenact a ritual of the adult world, as much as the college Fellows in Snow's *The Masters* work out the ritual of a power struggle in the larger world. Snow, however, gave his characters the knowledge attendant upon adulthood, while Golding by treating the boys' imagination as childish dilutes the seriousness of the theme. Without gaining the possible irony he intended, he partially dissipates the tremendous force of his narrative; the power that conflicting passions have generated dribbles away in the resolution.

(...)

The idea of a Golding novel invariably is superior to the performance itself. Ironically, the idea, often so engaging in the abstract, is self-defeating, for it forces an artificial method. Golding is an allegorist whose allegory pre-empts the realistic level; often, only the allegory is of interest and when that begins to wear thin, there is insufficient substance to grapple with.

Golding's novels, then, seem more attractive in their parts than as wholes. His inability, or lack of desire, to give intellectual substance to his themes, and his didactic intrusion in nearly all of the narratives, lessen the power of what still remains, however, an original talent. His eccentric themes, unfortunately, rarely convey the sense of balance and ripeness that indicate literary maturity: a shipwrecked sailor is interesting only if he is interesting; stranded boys are compelling only if their behavior indicates something significant about them and not merely their similarity to adults; an obsessed "loner" (like Sammy Mountjoy) is relevant only if he works out his problems in his own way without external influence, once it has been established that he is that kind of person; and pre-civilized people are attractive as literary material only if the author makes them act in some way that transcends their daily boredom, or if he can write about them ironically. To present all of these characters and situations "straight" is to take them as they are, and this evaluation simplifies them all out of proportion to what Golding's serious intentions demand.

To end a discussion of Golding's work on this note is, however, to lose sight of his importance to the contemporary novel. Even if his didacticism makes him resolve what should be unresolvable, he nevertheless indicates in nearly every line that he is an artist seriously interested in his craft. And even if he seems prone to surprise the reader with gimmicks, he nevertheless has demonstrated a sharp enough awareness of his material to overcome this defect before it permanently damages his fiction. When literary values overcome the moralist, Golding's potential may well be realized, and he will become an outstanding novelist.

Frank Kermode on William Golding and the 'Programme' of the Novel

If you dropped these boys into an Earthly Paradise 'they would not behave like God-fearing English gentlemen' but 'as like as not ... find savages who were kindly and uncomplicated ... The devil would rise out of the intellectual complications of the three white men.' Golding leaves the noble savages out of *Lord of the Flies* but this remark is worth quoting because it states the intellectual position in its basic simplicity. It is the civilized who are corrupt, out of phase with natural rhythm. Their guilt is the price of evolutionary success; and our awareness of this fact can be understood by duplicating Ballantyne's situation, borrowing his island, and letting his theme develop in this new and more substantial context. Once more every prospect pleases; but the vileness proceeds, not from cannibals, but from the boys, though Man is not so much vile as 'heroic and sick'. Unlike Ballantyne's boys, these are dirty and inefficient; they have some notion of order, symbolized by the beautiful conch which heralds formal meetings; but when uncongenial effort is required to maintain it, order disappears. The shelters are inadequate, the signal fire goes out at the very moment when Jack first succeeds in killing a pig. Intelligence fades; irrational taboos and blood-rituals make hopeless the task of the practical but partial intellect of Piggy; his glasses, the firemakers, are smashed and stolen, and in the end he himself is broken to pieces as he holds the conch. When civilized conditioning fades—how tedious Piggy's appeal to what adults might do or think!—the children are capable of neither savage nor civil gentleness. Always a little nearer to raw humanity than adults, they slip into a condition of animality depraved by mind, into the cruelty of hunters with their devil-liturgies and torture: they make an unnecessary, evil fortress, they steal, they abandon all operations aimed at restoring them to civility. Evil is the natural product of their consciousness. First the smallest boys create a beastie, a snake—'as if it wasn't a good island'. Then a beast is created in good earnest, and defined in a wonderful narrative sequence. The emblem of this evil society is the head of a dead pig, fixed, as a sacrifice, on the end of a stick and animated by flies and by the imagination of the *voyant*, Simon.

Simon is Golding's first 'saint, and a most important figure'. He is 'for the illiterate a proof of the existence of God' because the illiterate (to whom we are tacitly but unmistakably expected to attribute a correct insight here) will say, 'Well, a person like this cannot exist without a good God'. For Simon 'voluntarily embraces the beast ... and tries to get rid of him'. What he understands—and this is wisdom Golding treats with awe—is that evil is 'only us'. He climbs up to where the dead fire is dominated by the beast, a dead airman in a parachute, discovers what this terrible thing really is, and rushes off with the good news to the beach, where the maddened boys at their beast-slaying ritual mistake Simon himself for the beast and kill him. As Piggy, the dull practical intelligence, is reduced to blindness and futility, so Simon, the visionary, is murdered before he can communicate his comfortable knowledge. Finally, the whole Paradise is destroyed under the puzzled eyes of an adult observer. Boys will be boys.

The difference of this world from Ballantyne's simpler construction from similar materials is not merely a matter of incomparability of the two talents at work; our minds have, in general, darker needs and obscurer comforts. It would be absurd to suppose that the change has impoverished us; but it has seemed to divide our world into 'two cultures'—the followers of Jack and the admirers of Simon, those who build fortresses and those who want to name the beast.

Lord of the Flies was 'worked out carefully in every possible way', and its author holds that the 'programme' of the book is its meaning. He rejects Lawrence's doctrine, 'Never trust the artist, trust the tale' and its consequence, 'the proper function of the critic is to save the tale from the artist'. He is wrong, I think; in so far as the book differs from its programme there is, as a matter of common sense, material over which the writer has no absolute authority. This means not only that there are possible readings which he cannot veto, but even that some of his own views on the book may be in a sense wrong. The interpretation of the dead parachutist is an example. This began in the 'programme' as straight allegory; Golding says that this dead man 'is' History. 'All that we can give our children' in their trouble is this monstrous dead adult, who's 'dead, but won't lie down'; an ugly emblem of war and decay that broods over the paradise and provides the only objective equivalent for the beast the boys imagine. Now this limited allegory (I may even have expanded it in the telling) seems to me not to have got out of the 'programme' into the book; what does get in is more valuable because more like myth—capable, that is, of more various interpretation than the rigidity of Golding's scheme allows. And in writing of this kind all depends upon the author's mythopoeic power to transcend the 'programme'. Golding has this poetic power, and nowhere is it more impressively used than in his second book, *The Inheritors*.

Harry H. Taylor on the Case against William Golding's Simon-Piggy

Simon has been given the conventional characteristics of the mystic whose non-rational approach to the ways of knowing are presumably meant to re-assert the mystery and to re-affirm the meaning of the universe beyond its apparent basis in natural law but, in point of fact, Simon first fails to do so and then brings back the truth of the opposite. We have been led to believe in the possibility of the mystery which we later learn the author himself is not willing to accept but, on the other hand, cannot quite abandon. However, I think it is possible to suggest how this confusion has come about, and the other half of the dual hero, the fat boy Piggy, will make this clear.

If Simon represents intuition, feeling, the mystic's approach to knowledge, Piggy represents rationality, logic, science and the processes of thought on which ramatizesn depends. Piggy is the thinker behind the leader, Ralph. He is connected with fire; his glasses (a modern "invention") are used to start the fire in the first place and when he dies on the rock his death is somewhat Promethean. Further preoccupations stressing the importance of names, labels, scientific devices and the need for clock time set him apart from Simon, and clearly suggest his role as a rational and ramatizes force.

Simon's inordinate shyness and his difficulties with communication express his essential incompleteness. Piggy's asthma, nearsightedness and obesity express his incompleteness. These disabilities undoubtedly suggest the modern "wound", an image which has persisted from Conrad through Henry James, Hemingway and Faulkner. The wound reminds the reader that while Piggy possesses intelligence and a degree of morality, he is finally vulnerable because he has no sense of the "mystery" underlining all things. He is incapable of the kind of intuitive knowledge which is Simon's strong point.

(...)

"Which is better," Piggy finally shouts, "to have rules and agree, or to hunt and kill?" A few minutes afterwards, still holding the conch, Piggy is struck down by the boulder and dies below "across that square red rock in the sea". The death suggests sacrifice because of its Promethean overtones, and Piggy may also represent Icarus; Ralph remembers "the fall through the air of the true, wise friend called Piggy".

These symbols, unlike Simon's, will logically work for a figure who represents the decent man left alone in an empty universe. The death, bordering on the heroic, becomes a death given in gesture from the humanist's way of life, a humanism which can sometimes be maintained in the destructive element. It is, however, a death, and there is here no reference to resurrection, transfiguration, or the taking on of man's sins.[1]

Piggy, then, is the real central figure in the book because, despite his limiting blindness, it is his universe not Simon's, and nothing which happens to Piggy or to the symbols around him violates Golding's central symbol of the dead airman. If this is so, then Simon's mysticism should have been invalidated, or Simon himself should have been removed from the book in an early draft.

Why, then, does Golding insist upon Simon?

William Golding is emotionally committed to the non-rational approach as a valid part of human experience, but he is intellectually incapable of accepting what the mystic normally finds and, when the chips are down, he must lead the mystic saviour toward the author's own understanding of the universe.

Further, Piggy represents a vanishing breed of men which we have come to associate more closely with the last two centuries than with our own. He is the hopefully over-optimistic rationalist who assumes that man is a naturally reasonable creature and that, once scientific law has been fully understood, man will live in accordance with it a utopian life on earth. Piggy says that he "voted for no ghosts" (or the irrational element) not because he does not "believe" in the irrational element—he knows about psychiatrists—but because he finally assumes that the will-to-sanity is stronger than the will-to-destruction. In this sense, Piggy cannot grasp the meaning of historical facts like this century's two world wars, and to this degree he cannot cope with a horror like Jack, who through crude ritual celebrates the will-to-destruction.

But the trouble is that Piggy, by himself, ramatizes a rather shop-worn discovery—one which any reader of any sophistication takes for granted in this century, and another novel about over-optimistic rationalism will not make "a big book". Piggy, as hero (rather than Simon-Piggy), may very likely be the difference between comedy and tragedy. Golding knows that the important work still celebrates the mysteries, and ostensibly uses Simon to "enrich" his symbolism when, in fact, Simon's presence merely blurs it.

Note

1. Simon, when freeing the corpse from the wind's indignity, may be doing this.

EUGENE HOLLAHAN ON RUNNING IN CIRCLES: A MAJOR MOTIF IN *LORD OF THE FLIES*

As the foregoing analysis indicates, Golding's novel is arranged around the concept of two important kinds of circles, the first being the socio-political circle where the assembled boys engage in rational discussion in order to plan their way out of their difficulties, and the second being the tribal circle where the regressive boys dance ritually and kill savagely. On the whole, the first of the two great circles appears in the first half of the novel and the other in the second half. Conveniently, one might refer to these two group patterns as circle and anti-circle, although the terms might be only rhetorical and not essential. The social or civilized circle is established when the boys decide to conduct themselves along lines decreed by rational, democratic principles. When Ralph is elected leader, the "circle of boys broke into applause." The model they follow might be Parliament or any similar institution. Thereafter, whenever they meet upon the platform of pink granite thrusting out upon the beach from the forest, they automatically take their positions in a circle. Key episodes are thus highlighted by the circle form.

(...)

The tribal circle, or anti-circle, forms as a kind of reflex action from the disintegration of the more civilized circle on the platform. It is identified ultimately, of course, with another part of the island setting, Castle Rock. A foreshadowing of the violence and chanting linked with this circle occurs when the hunters excitedly relive their first kill. They describe how they had formed a circle, how they closed in on the pig, and then, when Maurice enters the ring pretending to be the victim: "Then Maurice pretended to be the pig and ran squealing into the centre, and the hunters, circling still, pretended to beat him. As they danced they sang" (p. 94). This innocent mimicry is later to become reality when the boys, having cast off Ralph's democratic common sense and Piggy's rationalism, revert to a primitive condition.

(...)

In summary, it seems hardly possible to overestimate the importance of the circle to Golding's purpose in *Lord of the Flies*. Artistically, it is perhaps the most significant motif; at least, it is a major one. As a recurrent motif, in its varied appearances, it carries with it many concepts of importance in the orchestration of Golding's complex theme. For example, as has been shown, in terms of the setting, the circle suggests both isolation and containment. In terms of several artifacts, it suggests rationalism and scientific progress as well as regression. With the characters, it is instrumental in showing extreme emotional states, defense mechanisms, persecutions, and taboos. As shown in relation to the entire group of boys, it suggests reason, order, civilization, integrity, while also showing change and disintegration. Violence and killing as manifested in tribal communal action are also represented by the circle. As Golding employs it, the circle represents both a rational arrangement and a primitive configuration. It is his main device for showing the shape of the two societies, or, put it another way, the two radical forms taken by the society on the island. The frequently-recurring circle images serve to remind the reader of the presence and importance of the two more important human circles, and the human configurations provide oblique commentary on the story in that they suggest that rational society and primitive tribe are in one sense fundamentally the same. In fact, the chief irony of the book, that Ralph's way and Jack's way take similar form, is conveyed by the circle image and motif.

KATHLEEN WOODWARD
ON AGGRESSION

But here I will not dwell on the book's aesthetic dimension except to call attention to a general problem in much commentary which takes analysis of symbolism as its point of departure: such criticism seems inevitably to falsify the character of *Lord of the Flies* by imputing interpretations to it whose weighty significance the straightforward text cannot support. Even the use of the term "symbolism" in regard to the book seems to me misguided—pretentious and overweaning. The refined techniques of New Criticism, so responsive to the intricacies of symbolist and modern poetry and the psychological and symbolic depth of a Melville or Faulkner novel, are inappropriate to the texture and scope of *Lord of the Flies*.

For example, it is quite evident just what the conch and the sow's head represent. There is a one-to-one correspondence between each literary sign and the political system to which it refers. By dubbing the sow's head "Lord of the Flies," which is a translation of the Hebrew *Ba'alzevuv* or the Greek *Beelzebub*, Golding alludes directly to the devil, or evil, in man. There is no mystery about this, no rich ambiguity of intent. It is a plain reference, plainly stated. Thus, when E. L. Epstein writes in notes to an edition of *Lord of the Flies* which is widely used in classrooms around the country, "Golding's Beelzebub is the modern equivalent, the anarchic, amoral, driving force that Freudians call the Id, whose only function seems to be to insure the survival of the host in which it is embedded or embodied, which function it performs with tremendous and single-minded tenacity," we find no parity between his interpretation and the text.[5] The former is far more sophisticated in terms of complexity of thought than the latter. Furthermore, Epstein's analysis allows him to inflate the significance of *Lord of the Flies* and mistakenly judge it to be one of the most important texts in the history of modern literature. He writes that in *Lord of the Flies*, "as in few others at the present time, are findings of psychoanalysts of all schools, anthropologists, social psychologists, and philosophical historians mobilized into an attack upon the central problem of modern thought: the nature of the human personality and the reflection of personality on society."[6] One would think Epstein were referring to another text altogether, for there is a strange air of unreality, an unmotivated profundity in his evaluation of *Lord of the Flies*. Although Golding's achievement is substantial, we must recognize that *Lord of the Flies* in no way possesses the ambitious and darkly troubled questioning of the human condition which we find in *Moby Dick* or *Heart of Darkness*. Indeed, Golding's book is literally small in scope: it is in reality a long short story rather than a short novel. And its systematic machinery, which drives the plot, operates impeccably and deliberately in a single direction. The text simply does not invite multiple and meaningful symbolic interpretations, no more than does *Brave New World* or *Walden Two*. For, like the authors of these books, Golding has set up, as it were, a fictional laboratory experiment whose outcome can be predicted with accuracy.

Notes
   5. "Notes on *Lord of the Flies*," in *Lord of the Flies*, p. 190.
   6. Epstein, pp. 189–90.

Golding's later novels, especially *The Pyramid* and *Rites of Passage*, make abundantly clear his deep bitterness at and hatred of the evils of class. But even in this first novel, even on a desert island, this Golding obsession is in evidence. The novelist Ian McEwan has written of his adolescent reading of *Lord of the Flies*: 'As far as I was concerned, Golding's island was a thinly disguised boarding school.'[20] At one point the narrator seems to claim that class is of no importance in the alienation and persecution of Piggy: 'There had grown up tacitly among the biguns the opinion that Piggy was an outsider, not only by accent, which did not matter, but by fat, and ass-mar, and specs, and a certain disinclination for manual labour' (p. 70). But the narrator implicitly admits that accent, a mark of class, is an alienating factor ['not only'] and actually mocks, in passing, Piggy's way of speaking. The view that class does not matter in Piggy's misfortunes is scarcely borne out by events. From the very outset Piggy is isolated, stranded on an island within the island, by being lower-class. On the book's first page Ralph's 'automatic gesture' of pulling up his socks makes 'the jungle seem for a moment like the Home Counties' (p. 7) and unfortunately Piggy just does not fit into the middle-class ambience implied thereby. Ralph is a good-natured boy, but in this initial scene he seems very reluctant to accept the friendship of the one companion he has so far found on the desert island: '"What's your name?" "Ralph." The fat boy waited to be asked his name in turn but this proffer of acquaintance was not made' (p. 9). One has the uncomfortable feeling throughout this scene that Ralph has been conditioned to be unfriendly towards boys who talk like Piggy. Ralph is not slow to inform Piggy that his father is officer-class, but in response to the crucial question '"What's your father?"' Piggy can produce only the poignant reply: '"My dad's dead," he said quickly, "and my mum—"' (p. 14). The unseemly haste with which Piggy announces that his father is dead suggests a reluctance to reveal his place in life and the blank after the mention of his mum speaks unhappy volumes. Piggy has failed to produce satisfactory credentials. It is at least partly for this reason that Piggy is doomed to become 'the centre of social derision so that everyone felt cheerful and normal' (p. 164). Life seems cheery and normal provided there are the likes of Piggy around to be looked down on and derided.

Piggy's main persecutor is Jack, who from the first evinces contempt and hatred for Piggy, whom he seems to regard as an upstart. Jack's education appears to have instilled in him the belief that it is his right to give commands, to rule: '"I ought to be chief," said Jack with simple arrogance, "because I'm chapter chorister and head boy"' (p. 23). His privileged choir-school background has no doubt taught him much about the necessity of hierarchies, including the notion that head boy from such a school ought to be top man anywhere. Whitley comments: 'This assumption of leadership, bred by being part of a civilised elite, is maintained when he becomes a member of a primitive elite. The perfect prefect becomes the perfect savage.'[21] It would be difficult to imagine anything more suggestive of innocence than a group of cathedral choristers, but we first see the choir as 'something dark' in the haze, as 'the darkness' (p. 20): the choir is from the outset associated with evil. A cathedral choir connotes also a certain English middle-class cosiness, a social world 'assured of certain certainties'. Here is Jack at his most 'sensible', declaring some important certainties: '"... We've got to have rules and obey them. After all, we're not savages. We're English; and the English are best at everything"' (p. 47). Golding has written that such cosy English chauvinism was something he particularly wished to attack in *Lord of the Flies*:

> One of our faults is to believe that evil is somewhere else and inherent in another nation. My book was to say: you think that now the war is over and an evil thing destroyed, you are safe because you are naturally kind and decent. (HG p. 89).

Notes

20. Ian McEwan, 'Schoolboys', in Carey, *William Golding*, p. 158.
21. Whitley, *Golding*, p. 28.
22. Tiger, *William Golding*, p. 51.

LAWRENCE S. FRIEDMAN ON THE INABILITY TO ALTER HUMAN NATURE

Barbarian pursuit, friendly ship, and miraculous rescue are no less present in Golding's conclusion. And when to these elements are added the hunt for sacrificial victims and the bloody rites of the Taurian religion, the resemblances between *Iphigenia in Tauris* and *Lord of the Flies* seem more than skin deep. Yet the lessons of the two works radically differ. Greek drama is ultimately conditioned by the proximity of the gods: omnipresent yet inscrutable they influence human action and determine human destiny. Since, as Sartre's Zeus admits, the gods need mortals for their worship as much as mortals need objects for their devotion, it follows that Greek drama chronicles this interdependence. In *The Flies*, Sartre's Zeus, the fading though still powerful king of the gods, owes his rule to human fear and superstition and relies upon man's willing servitude. When Orestes finally strides boldly into the sunlight, the spell of the gods is broken; henceforth he will blaze his own trail, acknowledging no law but his own. For Sartre, man's freedom begins with his denial of the gods and his full acceptance of responsibility for his actions and their consequences. And while existential freedom is as fearful as it is lonely, it is infinitely preferable to god-ridden bondage. Whether Dionysus stalking through *The Bacchae*, Athena watching over *Iphigenia in Tauris*, or Zeus brooding in *The Flies*, the gods play a role in the human drama. Note that all three deities carefully define their roles: Dionysus to punish the errant Thebans whose king denied him; Athena to ensure the proper worship of her sister, Artemis; and Zeus to warn the recalcitrant Orestes of the consequences of rebellion. So closely

73

are the gods involved with mortals that their interventions, no matter how arbitrary, take on a certain inevitable logic.

What Golding calls the "gimmicked" ending of *Lord of the Flies* and the Greek deus ex machina used most conventionally in *Iphigenia in Tauris* are alike in their technical function: to reverse the course of impending disaster. Yet their effects are quite different. Athena's wisdom is incontrovertible, her morality unassailable. High above the awed mortals she dispels chaos and imposes ideal order. The very fact of her appearance underlines the role of the gods in shaping human destiny. Golding's spiffy naval officer is, however, no god. Nor does he represent a higher morality. Confronted by the ragtag melee, he can only wonder that English boys hadn't put up a better show, and mistakes their savage hunt for fun and games à la *Coral Island*. While he cannot know the events preceding his arrival, his comments betray the same ignorance of human nature that contributed to the boys' undoing. Commanding his cruiser, the officer will direct a maritime search-and-destroy mission identical to the island hunt. *Lord of the Flies* ends with the officer gazing at the cruiser, preparing to reenact the age-old saga of man's inhumanity to man.

Just as the naval officer cannot measure up to Euripides' Athena, so Ralph falls short of Sartre's Orestes. Orestes strides into the sunlight of his own morality to live Sartre's dictum that existence precedes essence. Creating himself anew with each action, he will become his own god. Ralph can only weep for the loss of innocence from the world; he shows no particular signs of coping with his newfound knowledge. To understand one's nature is not to alter it. Morally diseased, mired in original sin, fallen man can rise only by the apparently impossible means of transcending his very nature. In man's apparent inability to re-create himself lies the tragedy of *Lord of the Flies*. The futility of Simon's sacrificial death, the failure of adult morality, and the final absence of God create the spiritual vacuum of Golding's novel. For Sartre the denial of the gods is the necessary prelude to human freedom. But for Golding, God's absence leads only to despair and human freedom is but license. "The theme of *Lord of the Flies* is grief, sheer grief, grief, grief."[11]

Note

11. Golding, "A Moving Target," p. 163.

STEFAN HAWLIN ON THE SAVAGES IN THE FOREST: DECOLONISING WILLIAM GOLDING

Lord of the Flies was published in 1954, in the middle of the period when Britain was beginning to give up Empire in a confused and reluctant way. 'Great' Britain's feelings of superiority were under threat, ruthlessly guarded in psychological and emotional terms but actually undermined by the pressure of nationalist movements and anti-colonial feeling. Later the official view was that Britain was engaged in 'the difficult and delicate politics of bringing new states to birth',[1] graciously withdrawing having helped to enlighten the dark places of the world. The ambivalence of feeling involved in the decolonisation process lies at the heart of *Lord of the Flies*, for the novel is defensive about the surrender of Empire, and makes an attempt to restate the old Empire misrepresentations of white enlightenment and black savagery. Under a thin disguise it presents the cliché about the bestiality and savagery of natives, the 'painted niggers' in the forest, ready at a whim to tear each other to pieces in tribal conflict unless the white 'grown-ups' come to rescue them from themselves. It is, in its odd way, a defence of colonialism.

The way the context of the 1950s has been largely ignored explains why the pattern above has gone unobserved, even though it exists on the surface of the text.[2] *Lord of the Flies* seems to make an eternally relevant point about human depravity, against progressivist views of humankind, but this point is well contained within the liberal consensus, and should hardly be shocking after Auschwitz and Hiroshima. This is Golding's own stated rationale. At first sight it seems so fair-minded that we need hardly see the problem involved:

Lord of the Flies was simply what it seemed sensible for me to write after the war, when everybody was thanking God they weren't Nazis. And I'd seen enough and thought enough to realize that every single one of us could be Nazis.... Nazi Germany was a particular kind of boil which burst in 1939. That was only the same kind of inflamed spot we all of us suffer from, and so I took English boys and said, 'Look. This could be you.' This is really what that book comes to.[3]

This seems unexceptionable, but there is a hint of naïvety: whoever really doubted that one nation was as capable of evil as another? Another account of the novel to the same interviewer reveals the implicit chauvinism. The discussion has come to centre on how a good arrangement of society— constitutionally, legally, and so forth—can help to create a good people. This is implicitly a celebration of the long evolution of the British constitution. What emerges is Golding's Empire-orientated view of the world, with England, America and a few other countries as places of light, and much of the rest of the world, particularly Africa, as below the level of civilisation. (Notice in the quotation the one-line caricature of 'savagery'.) From the nature of the remarks it is evident that Golding knows nothing substantial about Indian, African or Chinese culture, yet this does not stop him placing Britain— the centre of Empire, the centre of light!—at the top of a hierarchy of societies:

Aren't we giving too narrow a definition for society? I have been talking about the Western world. There *are* head-hunters still. There was Nazi Germany. There was Stalin's Russia. I don't know anything about China, but I'm prepared to believe anything you tell me about it. There are societies in India which do this, that, and t'other, and in Africa, et cetera, et cetera. I suppose what we are getting round to, finally, is the hopeless admission, in the middle of the twentieth century, that there is a hierarchy of society. The hierarchy of society must be based ultimately on a hierarchy of people. One can say that it is only by desperate efforts in one or two fortunate, or perhaps unfortunate, places on the surface of the globe that the bright side of man has been enabled to emerge even as dimly as it has, and this must be because of the nature of the people who built that society ...[4]

This perspective is not unusual for its time, but it is nonetheless strikingly expressed. Looking down from the top of the hierarchies of people (Britain), Golding does a quick survey of the dark realms of the earth—the realms to which, in the official ideology, the Empire sought to bring comfort and civilisation. As he looks out from this centre of light, many of the caricatures of Empire, of 'savages', unnatural cultural practices, tribal warfare, and so forth, float through his mind.

The English boys in *Lord of the Flies*, deposited on a desert island some time in the 1950s, descend slowly into depravity and atrocity—they become, in the loaded and often-repeated word of the text, 'savages'. Golding believes that he is showing us that the veneer of civilisation is very thin, that even (!) English boys might become little Nazis. The problem is that in discussing this Eurocentric revelation, this European-evolved evil, he takes his image of 'savagery' from the classic cultural misrepresentation (Empire-evolved) of white civilisation and black/African barbarity. The text shows us white, respectable, middle-class boys—whose fathers, incidentally, were the kind that governed the Empire centrally and locally—becoming like tribesmen, 'savages', or to put it in overtly racist terms, 'no better than blacks'. In depicting his primitives, Golding knows nothing serious about African mores and civilisation. His knowledge is at the level expressed in the remark 'there *are* head-hunters still'. He paints his savages from out of the paint-box of Empire myths, from pretty much the same paint-box as popular racist literature— Rider Haggard, John Buchan, Nicholas Monsarrat, for instance—literature which, as the Kenyan novelist Ngugi has expressed it, 'glorified imperialism and the deeds of its British actors while vilifying those of its opponents be they from rival imperialisms or from the native resistance'.[5] Another way of expressing this is to say that *Lord of the Flies* is a faint rewriting of Conrad's *Heart of Darkness*.

Notes

1. Margery Perham, *The Colonial Reckoning* (New York: Alfred Knopf, 1962), p. 24.

2. Even Alan Sinfield, in his brief discussion of Golding, seeing *Lord of the Flies* primarily in opposition to *The Coral Island*, only concludes that 'Golding's distinct post-colonial inflection is to attribute savagery, in principle, to the British ruling élite' (p. 142), but he does not begin to question this idea of savagery. See *Literature, Politics and Culture in Postwar Britain* (Oxford: Blackwell, 1989), pp. 141ff.

3. Jack I. Biles, *Talk: Conversations with William Golding* (New York: Harcourt Brace Jovanovich, 1970), pp. 3–4.

4. Ibid., p. 45.

5. Ngugi wa Thiong'o, *Moving the Centre: The Struggle for Cultural Freedoms* (London: James Currey, 1993), p. 140.

JAMES R. BAKER ON GOLDING AND HUXLEY: THE FABLES OF DEMONIC POSSESSION

In 1962 I began correspondence with Golding in preparation for a book on his work (*William Golding: A Critical Study*). My thesis, foreshadowed in an essay published in 1963 ("Why It's No Go"), was that the structure and spirit of *Lord of the Flies* were modeled on Euripidean tragedy, specifically *The Bacchae*, and that the later novels also borrowed character and structure from the ancient tragedians. Golding's response to the book was positive, kinder than I expected, but it carried a hint I did not immediately understand:

> With regard to Greek, you are quite right that I go to that literature for its profound engagement with first and last things. But though a few years ago it was true I'd read little but Greek for twenty years, it's true no longer. The Greek is still there and I go back to it when I feel like that; now I must get in touch with the contemporary scene, and not necessarily the literary one; the scientific one perhaps. (Baker and Golding, letter 12 August 1965)

Science? What could he mean? *Lord of the Flies* and *The Inheritors*, as many readers recognized, had displayed a broad knowledge of anthropological literature. *Pincher Martin*, the third novel, was not such an obvious case, but it did focus on an arrogant rationalist who repudiated any belief in a god and claimed for himself the god-like power to create his own world, his own virtual reality. *Free Fall* (1959) had more obviously employed scientific metaphor—the state of free fall or freedom from gravitational law—to describe the moral drift and lawlessness of the narrator, Sammy Mountjoy; and his mentor, the science teacher Nick Shales, is found in Sammy's retrospective search for pattern in his life to be an incredibly one-sided and façade man. And the little comic play, *The Brass Butterfly* (1958), satirized the ancient Greek scientist Phanocles, a brilliant but dangerously destructive inventor who specializes in explosive devices. Was Piggy, the precocious protoscientist of *Lord of the Flies*, first in this series of negative and satirical portraits? At the urging of his father, a devotee of science, Golding had gone up to Oxford in 1930 to study science, but after two years he threw it over to study literature. Some of the student poems written at Oxford, published in 1934, mock the rationalist's faith that order rules our experience, and these seem to evidence that turning point. Years later he wrote a humorous autobiographical sketch, "The Ladder and the Tree" (1965), recalling the conflict that had troubled him as he prepared to enter the university. The voice of his father joined with Einstein and Sir James Jeans (and no doubt the authors of all those scientific classics found in the household), while the voice of Edgar Allan Poe, advocate for darkness and mystery, urged him to choose the alternative path.

When I interviewed Golding in 1982 I was determined to question him about this early confrontation with the two cultures. Had there been a "classic revolt," I asked, against his father's scientific point of view? After some defense of the father's complexity of mind, the conclusion was clear: "But I do think that during the formative years I did feel myself to be in a sort of rationalist atmosphere against which I kicked" (130).

(...)

Though Huxley was mentor and guide for many of the ideas and devices that went into Golding's allegory, *Lord of the Flies* offers no real hope for redemption.[6] Golding kills off the only saint available (as history obliges him to do) and demonstrates the inadequacy of a decent leader (Ralph) who is at once too innocent and ignorant of the human heart to save the day from darkness. In later years Golding struggled toward a view in which science and the humanities might be linked in useful partnership, and he tried to believe, as Huxley surely did, that the visible world and its laws were the façade of a spiritual realm. He realized something of this effort in the moral thermodynamics of *Darkness Visible* (1974) and again, somewhat obscurely, in the posthumous novel *The Double Tongue* (1995). His Nobel speech asserts that the bridge between the visible and invisible worlds, one he failed to find in the earlier *Free Fall*, does in fact exist. Thus both novelists recovered to some degree from the trauma of disillusionment with scientific humanism suffered during the war, and both aspired to hope that humanity would somehow evolve beyond the old tragic flaws that assured the rebirth of the devil in every generation.

Note

6. In a letter to his brother, Sir Julian Huxley, 9 June 1952, Huxley counters the idea that there can be no redemption for fallen man:

> Everything seems to point to the fact that, as one goes down through the subliminal, one passes through a layer (with which psychologists commonly deal) predominantly evil and making for evil—a layer of "Original Sin," if one likes to call it so—into a deeper layer of "Original Virtue," which is one of peace, illumination, and insight, which seems to be on the fringes of Pure Ego or Atman. (*Letters* 635–36)

One of the most powerful carnivalesque elements in *Lord of the Flies* is that of the pig, which Golding uses symbolically to subvert dominant racial assumptions, in particular toward the Jews, and, universally, toward those humans considered alien or foreign to any grouping. This has alarming relevance to the atrocities committed against the Jews in World War II, yet has been overlooked by Golding critics who have not interpreted Golding's merging of the pig hunt with the human hunt, and the racial significance of eating pig flesh at carnival time.

The pig symbol is developed in *Lord of the Flies* as the pig of carnival time. It is a major motif: as locus of projected evil; as food for the schoolboys; as propitiation to the Beast; but more than anything, as the meat the Jews do not eat. This link between pig flesh and the Jews is reinforced by Golding's choice of the novel's Hebraic title. "Lord of the Flies," or "Lord of Dung," as John Whitley renders it, comes from the Hebrew word *Beelzebub*. As I noted earlier, Peter Stallybrass and Allon White argue that the eating of pig meat during carnival time is an anti-Semitic practice. It is an act of contempt toward the Jews for bringing about the Lenten fast. White asserts: "Meat, especially, pig meat, was of course the symbolic centre of carnival (*carne levare* probably derives from the taking up of meat as both food and sex)." That the pig becomes human and the human being becomes pig in the frenzied, carnivalistic debauchery of Jack and his totalitarian regime is important. The shadowing of pig hunt and human hunt, ending with Simon's and Piggy's deaths, and almost with Ralph's, signifies the link between the pig symbol and the extermination of those considered alien or outsiders. The name "Piggy" does not merely imply obesity. It is the lower-class Piggy who is always on the periphery of the group of schoolboys, always mocked, never quite belonging. As Virginia Tiger points out, "Piggy is killed ... because he is an alien, a pseudo-species."[18] Piggy is alien or foreign, and, as such, he is a focus for violence based on the sort of racial assumptions found in Ballantyne's writing, but it is important to clarify the precise nature of his outsider status. The character name "Piggy" does not, unlike that of Ralph and Jack, feature in Ballantyne's *Coral Island*. Piggy is Golding's creation—a creation that suggests a Jew-like figure: "There had grown tacitly among the biguns the opinion that Piggy was an outsider, not only by accent, which did not matter, but by fat, and ass-mar, and specs, and a certain disinclination for manual labour" (*LF*, 70). We find something of the Jewish intellectual in this description of the bespectacled Piggy, with his different accent and physical feebleness. The stereotype of Jewish feebleness has been a stock in trade of anti-Semites and peddlers of degeneration theories.[19] It is here that we witness the anti-Semitism of carnival. In essence, Golding utilizes the imperial tradition of pig sticking to suggest a continuum between English imperialism and fascism.

Jack's gang persecutes Jew-like Piggy and those it considers outsiders. As a carnival mob they break the normal rules of authority with a willful, transgressive violence that marks a shift from liberal democracy to fascism and anti-Semitism. We witness the demise of Ralph's parliament and the ascendancy of Jack's totalitarian, primitive regime based on savagery, hunting, and primal drives. There follows aggressive sexual debasement and frenzy in the killing of the carnival pig.

Notes

18. Whitley, Golding: *"Lord of the Flies,"* 43; see Stallybrass and White, *Politics of Transgression*, 54; White, *Carnival, Hysteria and Writing*, 170; Tiger, *Dark Fields*, 63.

19. See Sander Gilman, *Franz Kafka: The Jewish Patient*. See also Gilman, *The Jew's Body*.

Works by William Golding

Poems, 1934.
Lord of the Flies, 1954.
The Inheritors, 1955.
Pincher Martin, 1956.
The Brass Butterfly, 1958.
Free Fall, 1959.
The Spire, 1964.
The Hot Gates and Other Occasional Pieces, 1965.
The Pyramid, 1967.
Talk: Conversations with William Golding (with Jack I. Biles), 1970.
The Scorpion God: Three Short Novels, 1971.
Darkness Visible, 1979.
Rites of Passage, 1980.
A Moving Target, 1982.
The Paper Men, 1984.
An Egyptian Journal, 1985.
Close Quarters, 1987.
Fire Down Below, 1989.
The Double Tongue, 1995.

Annotated Bibliography

Babb, Howard. *"Lord of the Flies."* In *The Novels of William Golding*. Columbus: Ohio State University Press, 1970.

Babb sees many of the critics as incorrect in their focus on the meaning of the novel and in ignoring the novel's "artistry in narrative." To combat this perspective, he describes the narrative structures in the book, then examines the characters, and then using one scene attempts to show how "the method of the novel is realized in its language."

Baker, James, R. "Why It's No Go," *Arizona Quarterly* 19 (Winter 1963).

Baker disagrees with critics who categorize *Lord of the Flies* with works of Conrad or *Robinson Crusoe*. Instead, he comments on Golding's being influenced by classical Greek literature, especially Euripides' *The Bacchae*. Similarly, he points out that critics have too readily categorized Golding as being indebted to Christian sources and appearing as a Christian moralist. Instead, he says, Golding satirizes both the Christian and rationalist viewpoints.

Baker, James, R. and Arthur P. Ziegler, Jr., eds. *Lord of the Flies* (Casebook Edition). New York: Berkley Publishing Group, 1988.

This book contains the complete novel as well as two interviews with Golding, a letter about *Lord of the Flies* by Golding's brother, and twelve essays, all but one of which were previously printed and some of which have been revised. These explore psychological, religious, and literary views of the novel, and compare the text to earlier Golding work as well as to other novels. Included is a bibliography as well.

Dickson, L.L. *"Lord of the Flies."* In *The Modern Allegories of William Golding*. Tampa: University of South Florida Press, 1990.

Dickson points out four levels of meaning operating in the novel. First there is the psychological dimension that shows Ralph, Jack, and Piggy as symbols of the three-part human psyche composed of the ego, id, and superego. Second, there are archetypal patterns—the quest motif, the Dionysian myth. Third, there is a reference to the two main characters, representing democracy and totalitarianism. Fourth, there is a moral allegory showing conflicts between good and evil.

Gindin, James. "The Fictional Explosion: *Lord of the Flies* and *The Inheritors*." In *William Golding*. New York: St. Martin's Press, 1988.

Gindin addresses what others and Gindin himself have discussed about *Lord of the Flies*—whether it can be categorized into fable or the higher category of myth. Gindin compares *Lord of the Flies* to Golding's *The Inheritors* and says that both works stand as unique works. He explains that from these Golding creates his own form, building on religious and literary tradition. This work, *Pincher Martin*, he calls Golding's "unique and symbolic literary explosion."

Hodson, Leighton. "The Metaphor of Darkness: *Lord of the Flies*." In *William Golding*. Edinburgh: Oliver & Boyd, 1969.

Hodson espouses the view that readers are too intent on easily categorizing and deciphering the message Golding is voicing through the novel. Holden cites that too many have mistakenly seen *Lord of the Flies* as providing a view of complete blackness in man, which he says prevents the reader from seeing its true complexity and literary worth.

Johnston, Arnold. "*Lord of the Flies*: Fable, Myth, and Fiction." In *Of Earth and Darkness: The Novels of William Golding*. Columbia: University of Missouri Press, 1980.

Johnston looks at what he sees as the two connected but separate threads that run through the novel—the actual narrative that shows the boys becoming savages and the symbol of the beast that at first seems nothing more than an outgrowth of the youngest boys's nightmares and then comes to stand for the dark side residing in all. Johnston admits that at times Golding is heavy-handed in trying to relay a message but believes this does not overpower the novelist's other skills as a fiction writer.

Kinkead-Weekes, Mark. "*Lord of the Flies*." In *William Golding, A Critical Study*, edited by Mark Kinkead-Weekes and Ian Gregor. London: Faber & Faber, 1967.

These authors explain why *Lord of the Flies* has retained its remarkable appeal—"its powerful and exciting qualities as narrative, and its appearance of extreme clarity of meaning." They argue that while Golding's later works deserve more attention, these books don't get that because of the greater difficulty they present in reading and understanding. From here, though, the authors argue that the public's view of *Lord of the Flies* as clear in meaning may actually be off the mark.

Niemeyer, Carl. "The Coral Island Revisited," *College English* 22, no. 4 (January 1961).

While numerous critics compare *Lord of the Flies* to R. M. Ballantyne's *The Coral Island*, few do it as extensively as Niemeyer, whose essay is frequently cited by others. Not only is the comparison between the two novels made by critics but it is made by characters in Golding's book as well. These characters seem to think highly of the Coral Island story, and at least one believes it is indicative of how humanity behaves. Ballantyne himself said it was a true story, and its pleasant characters and events starkly contrast it to Golding's symbolic story of boys' intrinsically bad selves let loose.

Rosenfield, Claire. "'Men of a Smaller Growth': A Psychological Analysis of William Golding's *Lord of the Flies*," *Literature and Psychology* 11, no. 4 (Autumn 1961): pp. 93–100.

Rosenfield shows Golding's use of Freudian theory yet argues that the meanings of the novel are not so clear or simple. The book's goal, in her view, is not only a re-creation of Freud's perspective that children are small savages rather than innocents. Beyond this, Rosenfield writes, Golding comments on the adult world as well, itself damaged by war and primitive and irrational.

Swisher, Clarice, ed. *Readings on* Lord of the Flies. San Diego: Greenhaven, 1997.

Swisher gathers together a large collection of essays on the novel covering topics such as significant motifs in the text, its deliberately obscure setting, the use of irony, whether it should be categorized as literature, and its "unwarranted" popularity.

Whitley, John S. Golding: *Lord of the Flies*. London: Edward Arnold Ltd., 1970.

Whitley explores how the work fits in as a fable, the realism of the boys and their speech, Golding's use of symbolism, the beast and violence on the island, and the controversial ending. Additionally, he spends time on foreshadowings, which other critics lightly touch on. The book includes a bibliography.

Contributors

Harold Bloom is Sterling Professor of the Humanities at Yale University. He is the author of over 20 books, including *Shelley's Mythmaking* (1959), *The Visionary Company* (1961), *Blake's Apocalypse* (1963), *Yeats* (1970), *A Map of Misreading* (1975), *Kabbalah and Criticism* (1975), *Agon: Toward a Theory of Revisionism* (1982), *The American Religion* (1992), *The Western Canon* (1994), and *Omens of Millennium: The Gnosis of Angels, Dreams, and Resurrection* (1996). *The Anxiety of Influence* (1973) sets forth Professor Bloom's provocative theory of the literary relationships between the great writers and their predecessors. His most recent books include *Shakespeare: The Invention of the Human* (1998), a 1998 National Book Award finalist, *How to Read and Why* (2000), *Genius: A Mosaic of One Hundred Exemplary Creative Minds* (2002), and *Hamlet: Poem Unlimited* (2003). In 1999, Professor Bloom received the prestigious American Academy of Arts and Letters Gold Medal for Criticism, and in 2002 he received the Catalonia International Prize.

Pamela Loos has written and/or researched more than 35 books of Literary Criticism, covering authors ranging from Goethe to Cormac McCarthy. She is the project editor of *Women Memorists, Vol. II.*

William Golding wrote numerous books and won the Nobel Prize for literature in 1983. He was writer-in-residence at Hollins College from 1961–62 and thereafter worked at his writing full time.

E.M. Forster, one of the most significant British novelists of the twentieth century, was also a leading critic and reviewer. Among his key critical works are *Abinger Harvest* and *Aspects of the Novel.*

Frederick R. Karl teaches English at New York University and is the writer or editor of several works, such as *A Reader's Guide to Joseph Conrad* and *George Eliot: Voice of a Century*.

Frank Kermode is an eminent English critic who taught at numerous universities, including Harvard, Cambridge, and Columbia. He is the editor of *The Oxford Anthology of English Literature* and the author or editor of approximately forty additional titles.

Harry H. Taylor has taught at American University. He has written three books and also has published essays in critical journals.

Eugene Hollahan has taught at Georgia State University. He is the author of *Crisis-Consciousness and the Novel* and the author or editor of books on Gerard Manley Hopkins and Saul Bellow.

Kathleen Woodward teaches English at the University of Washington. She is the author of *Questioning Identity: Gender Class Nation* and the editor or author of other titles as well.

S. J. Boyd has been Lecturer of English at the University of St. Andrews and is the author of *The Novels of William Golding*.

Lawrence S. Friedman has written a book on William Golding and also published books on Cynthia Ozick and Isaac Bashevis Singer.

Stefan Hawlin has been a Professor in the Department of English Studies at the University of Buckingham. He is the co-author of two volumes of *The Poetical Works of Robert Browning* and also has edited and written other books on Browning.

James R. Baker is the author or joint editor of a few books on William Golding as well as of other titles. He is one of the founders of the journal *Twentieth Century Literature*.

Paul Crawford has been a lecturer at the University of Nottingham. He is the author of *Politics and History in William Golding: The World Turned Upside Down* and also has published a novel.

Acknowledgments

"Fable" by William Golding. From *The Hot Gates and Other Occasional Pieces*: 86–88, 89. © 1961, 1962, 1963, 1965 by William Golding. Reprinted by permission of Harcourt, Inc.

"Introduction" by E. M. Forster. From *Lord of the Flies*: xi–xii, xiii. © 1962 by Cord-McCann, Inc.; © 1954 by William Golding. Reprinted by permission of Penquin Group (USA).

"The Metaphysical Novels of William Golding" by Frederick R. Karl. From *The Contemporary English Novel*: 257, 258, 259–260. © 1962 by Frederick Karl. Reprinted by permission of Farrar, Straus and Giroux LLC.

"William Golding" by Frank Kermode. From *Puzzles and Epiphanies*: 203–205. © 1962 by Frank Kermode. Reprinted by permission of Taylor and Francis Books, Ltd.

"The Case Against William Golding's Simon-Piggy" by Harry H. Taylor. From *Contemporary Review* 209, no. 1208 (September 1966): 157–158, 159–160. © 1966 by Contemporary Review Co. Ltd. Reprinted by permission from Contemporary Review.

"Running in Circles: A Major Motif in *Lord of the Flies*" by Eugene Hollahan. From *Studies in the Novel* 2, no. 1 (Spring 1970): pp. 26–27, 29. © 1970 by North Texas State University. Reprinted by permission.

"On Aggression: William Golding's *Lord of the Flies*" by Kathleen Woodward. From *No Place Else: Explorations in Utopian and Dystopian Fiction*, edited by Eric S. Rabkin, Martin H. Greenberg, Joseph D. Olander: 200–202. © 1983 by the Board of Trustees, Southern Illinois University. Reprinted by permission.

Index